The Free and

Cookbook

By Carole Kruppa

Surrey Books
500 N. Michigan Ave.
Suite 1940
Chicago, IL 60611

THE FREE AND EQUAL® COOKBOOK is published by Surrey Books, Inc., 500 N. Michigan Ave., Chicago, IL 60611

This book is manufactured in the United States of America.

ISBN: 09609516-5-2

Library of Congress Cataloging in Publication Data:

Kruppa, Carole.
  The Free and Equal® Cookbook.

  Includes index.
  1. Low-calorie diet—Recipes. 2. Sugar substitutes.
I. Title.
RM222.2.K78 1985   641.5'635   85-2626
ISBN 0-9609516-5-2

        6 7 8 9 10

Design and production by Cynthia Hoffman Design, Chicago.
Illustrations by Cynthia Hoffman.

Single copies may be ordered by sending check or money order for $7.50 postpaid to Surrey Books at the above address. For orders of 100 or more copies, please contact the publisher for special discounts.

Dedication

To my husband for his patience and willingness to taste...

To my mother and grandmother who instilled in me a taste for fine food...

To my father-in-law who contributed this poem:

> *Give yourself an Equal® chance*
> *To receive many an envious glance.*
> *Just follow the recipes in this book —*
> *You'll like it, if you only look.*

To dieters everywhere...Bon Appétit!

Acknowledgments

The author would like to thank the following people who were responsible in part for the publication of this book:

Editorial consultant Nao Hauser; copy editor Sara Steinberg; editorial assistant Debra Schwartz; Joan Booz of Cynthia Hoffman Design; Virginia Barber of Total Typography; Bertha Curl of Bookcrafters, Inc.; Nadine Richterman; and Lily Stag, typist extraordinaire.

Foreword

A curious experiment turned into a priceless evening. It had all started a week earlier when Carole Kruppa called me at my office in downtown Chicago.

"Marty," she said, "I've written a cookbook called The Free and Equal® Cookbook. The recipes use Equal® in place of sugar, most are low-fat, low cholesterol, and low salt. All milk is skim. There's no butter; vegetable spray replaces oil and is polyunsaturated. The egg yolk contents of recipes can be cut in half. Would you be willing to write a foreward?"

Skeptical me, I wondered, "Low calorie and no sugar. But what about fat, cholesterol and salt? Could such recipes be healthful for diabetics, people with high blood fats or patients with arteriosclerosis?"

"OK, Carole, I'll make you a deal," I said. "Let me review the manuscript and then let's experiment. Invite my wife Renée and me for a dinner made entirely from your recipes. We won't tell Renée anything. She's pretty fussy about food, so let's see how it really tastes, and then I'll decide about writing an introduction."

The night for our experiment was a cold, snowy Friday in February. The door opened to a cheerful, crackling log fire and a warm greeting from Carole and her husband Harvey and another old friend, Bryan Ackerman. As we reminisced beside the fire, I'd already eaten three crackers spread with Carole's Salmon Ball appetizer before I remembered that it was "diet food." Renée looked like she was enjoying it. Did Bryan know?

Dinner was served with panâche. The Wilted Spinach Salad and Cioppino soup were a gourmet's preview for the main attractions of Shrimp Creole and Baby Carrots à l'Orange. Strangely enough, we were overstuffed when the dessert, Espresso Parfait Cheesecake, arrived. It was delicious and light and capped one of the nicest meals I'd ever had.

After dinner we relaxed as Harvey, a professional pianist, warmed us with his considerable talent. We didn't slip away until 1:30 a.m.

In the car on the way home Renée asked, "Do you think Carole would give me those recipes?" Enough said. Wait 'till Renée finds out our elegant meal was a "diet dinner," made with Equal®. I'll call Carole tomorrow and tell her I'll write that introduction.

I. Martin Grais, M.D.
Clinical Cardiology Group, Ltd.
Chicago, Illinois

Contents

Introduction

Ahhh, chocolate mousse, a thick shake, cheesecake—
wouldn't they taste great right now? You will discover as you
flip through *The Free and Equal® Cookbook* that these and
other treats can be enjoyed while dieting. If you are dieting
to lose weight, or just wish to reduce sugar consumption
and have no dietary restrictions beyond controlling your
weight, this book was written for you.

Dieting is fun, really—once you get the knack, it becomes
a game. Approach the task with a light spirit; there is
hardly anything more satisfying than losing unwanted
weight while enjoying every meal.

This book answers two different questions about dieting.
The first is the nuts-and-bolts "How to?" How do you prepare low-calorie food that is eye-appealing, delicious, and
quick or easy to make? What are some innovative ways of
getting the most from available low-calorie ingredients? For
these purposes, *The Free and Equal® Cookbook* offers
scores of tempting recipes for everything from hit-the-spot
snacks to glorious desserts.

The second question is a more personal one: "How do I
diet without the added work and expense of preparing two
meals—one for myself and one for the rest of the family? I
am so busy that preparing special food for myself would
take too much time." *The Free and Equal® Cookbook* contains recipes your whole family will love. These include
such traditional favorites as saucy franks, stuffed peppers,
and cream puffs, as well as many dishes that will become
new favorites. You will be able to cook once, and for all.

Whichever approach speaks more strongly to you, I rec-
ommend that you read through the entire book before
turning to a specific recipe. Then you will realize that dieting

does not mean the end of good eating.

Growing up as I did, in a French family, I developed a life-long liaison with good food. It continues, despite my recent need to count calories. I say recent, because turning forty made me realize that nothing—including youthful slimness—lasts forever. As a result, I began to look at ways to reduce calories in the foods I love, while not sacrificing taste. So began my adventure into low-calorie cooking.

I discovered that while many ingredients contribute greatly to recipes, providing both nutrition and taste, sugar is one that adds mostly empty calories. So I began using Equal®* brand sweetener to add a bit of sweetness to other low-calorie ingredients. One packet of Equal® provides the sweetness of two teaspoons of sugar and contains only four calories, compared to the thirty-two calories of the two teaspoons of sugar. Artificial sweeteners are available, but their unpleasant aftertaste often overpowers the natural flavor of food. Equal® is different from other low-calorie sweeteners because it contains NutraSweet®* brand sweetener, a sweetening ingredient made from protein components like those found naturally in many foods. Equal® does not contain saccharin or sodium.

This book includes recipes for breakfast treats, appetizers, soups, salads, entrées, desserts, beverages, and jams. These recipes are designed for use with Equal®; results will be different if other sweeteners are substituted. Cooking with Equal® does have some limitations. For example, Equal® is not recommended for baking because it does not provide the bulk and structure of sugar, and prolonged exposure to oven or range heat will diminish its sweetness. However, I haven't let this prevent me from using Equal® to create marvelous cakes, pies, and desserts; I just devised techniques that allow me to add the sweetener after baking or in other ways.

I think it's especially important when dieting to eat the foods you love. With the recipes in this book, you should feel free to do so any time. You can serve almost any of the appetizers, soups, salads, or entrées as either a first course or a main course. The breakfast fare might tempt you at supper time. And some of the light desserts and beverages

*Equal® and NutraSweet® are registered trademarks of G. D. Searle & Co. Searle has neither sponsored nor is otherwise connected with this publication.

would be delightful for breakfast. So, dig in and enjoy!

One mealtime pleasure I feel strongly about is the appearance of the table. You'll find this concern reflected in the many garnishing suggestions I've included with the recipes. Meals can be further enhanced by attention to such details as color-coordinated place-settings, fresh flowers, or even an artfully arranged centerpiece of fresh fruits and vegetables. I encourage you to use your imagination. Feel free to banish boredom from your meals. Use *The Free and Equal®️ Cookbook* to play the dieting game. Begin now. The numbers are in your favor!

Carole Kruppa

Appetizers
and Snacks

As I planned this chapter the word "nosh" kept dancing in my head. I delight in trying a bite of this or a morsel of that—you might even say it's my favorite pastime! So appetizers are the most fun to think about, since they offer great opportunities for noshing.

They also lend themselves to artistic presentations. I like to set an array of appetizers on a buffet like a beautiful mosaic, garnished to please both the eye and the palate. Often I use their delicate colors and shapes to offset other foods. Imagine the soft pink of a Salmon fish mold next to the pale green of My Favorite Cole Slaw (see Index), or the plump shape of a pumpkin filled with Golden Carrot Soup contrasted with delicate seafood-filled Cream Puffs.

Many of the dishes presented here can be served as dinner first courses or as luncheon or light supper entrées. Some are quickly made "little nothings"—perfect for the times when a friend drops in for a glass of wine and a chat. Best of all, these recipes can be enjoyed on your diet anytime—so you need never be deprived of a nosh!

Light and refreshing—a great way to start a summer meal.

Fresh Orange Juice Delight

1½ teaspoons unflavored gelatin
¼ cup warm water
2 cups freshly squeezed orange juice
1 packet of Equal®
Grated rind of 1 orange

Soften the gelatin in warm water. Combine the orange juice and gelatin with Equal®. Refrigerate until jelled. Cut the gelatin into small cubes and serve in champagne glasses. Garnish with the grated orange rind.

Makes 4 servings.
Calories: 41 per serving.

Broiled Grapefruit

2 medium grapefruits, cut in half
2 tablespoons dry sherry
2 packets Equal®

Using a grapefruit knife, separate the flesh of the grapefruits from the shell and separate into sections, making sure they are loosened from the peel. Sprinkle with sherry and broil until the grapefruits are slightly brown and the tops glazed. Remove from the oven and sprinkle with Equal®. The alcohol in the sherry evaporates during broiling so no calories are added.

2

Makes 4 servings.
Calories: 41 per serving.

The ginger dressing gives this appetizer special appeal.

Citrus Supreme with Zesty Ginger Dressing

12 grapefruit sections
12 orange sections
4 crisp lettuce cups
Zesty Ginger Dressing (recipe follows)

Place 3 grapefruit sections and 3 orange sections in each lettuce cup. Prepare ginger dressing. Spoon 1 tablespoon dressing over citrus.

Makes 4 servings.
Calories: 80 per serving.

Zesty Ginger Dressing:

1 cup cottage cheese
2 tablespoons skim milk
3 packets Equal®
¼ cup sour cream
1 tablespoon orange juice
6 teaspoons grated orange peel
2 teaspoons minced candied ginger

Place cottage cheese, milk, and Equal® in blender. Process till smooth. Add sour cream and remaining ingredients except candied ginger. Blend till smooth. Stir in candied ginger.

Makes 8 servings; 43 calories each.

3

Everyone will love these spicy little morsels.

Saucy Franks

> 1 pound cocktail franks
> 2 tablespoons diet margarine
> 2 tablespoons cornstarch
> ⅔ cup chicken broth
> ⅔ cup red wine vinegar
> 4 tablespoons frozen concentrated
>   pineapple juice
> 4 tablespoons chopped pimiento
> 2 tablespoons soy sauce
> ½ teaspoon garlic powder
> ½ teaspoon ground ginger
> 4 packets Equal®

Sauté franks in margarine for about 5 minutes. Set aside. Combine cornstarch and chicken broth in small saucepan. Stir in remaining ingredients except Equal®. Cook over medium heat, stirring until thickened and bubbly. Remove from heat and stir in Equal®. Place franks in sauce and let stand for about 2 minutes. Place in serving dish surrounded by toothpicks.

Makes 8 servings, 3 franks each.
Calories: 89 per serving.

Tip: You can use 1 pound lean ground beef for tiny meatballs.

This shrimp cocktail is special because it looks beautiful and tastes wonderful.

4 Shrimp Cocktail Supreme

> 1 bottle (11 ounces) dietetic ketchup (no
>   sugar or salt added)
> 1 tablespoon fresh lemon juice
> 2 packets Equal®

¼ cup horseradish
4 medium green peppers
½ cup chopped green pepper
¼ cup chopped chives (optional)
16 medium shrimp, cooked and chilled

Mix ketchup, lemon juice, Equal®, and horseradish. (Adjust horseradish and lemon juice to taste.) Add chopped green pepper. Refrigerate till well chilled. Meanwhile, cut the tops off the peppers and remove all seeds and pulp. Arrange a pepper shell on a small plate. Take 4 shrimp for each serving and hang them on the edge of the pepper shell all around the opening. Add 2 tablespoons of dressing over the top and garnish with chives before serving. Serve very cold.

Makes 4 servings.
Calories: 80 per serving.

A nice way to begin an elegant meal.

Smoked Salmon Cream Cheese Rolls

¼ pound smoked salmon (lox), sliced
thin (about four 1-oz. slices)
1 package (4 ounces) low-calorie cream
cheese, softened and mixed with
1 packet Equal®
2 tablespoons capers, chopped
4 large romaine lettuce leaves
Lemon wedges

Spread very thin slices of smoked salmon with caper-studded cream cheese; roll up jelly-roll fashion. Cut rolls in ½-inch slices. Place a romaine leaf on a plate. Place 5 salmon rounds in a row down the center of the leaf. Garnish with a lemon wedge.

5

Makes 4 servings.
Calories: 116 per serving.

A festive way to start a barbecue or a party .

Oriental Skewered Shrimp

¾ cup medium dry California sherry
¼ cup soy sauce
½ teaspoon ground ginger
36 raw medium shrimp, shelled and
  deveined (about 1¼ pounds)
Wooden or bamboo skewers, about
  9 inches long
Cherry tomatoes
Yellow pickled peppers
1 packet Equal®

Combine sherry, soy sauce, and ginger. Heat just to boiling. Remove from heat. Cool to room temperature. Wash shrimp. Thread 3 shrimp lengthwise, through the center, heads doubled up against the tails of each skewer. Thread cherry tomato or yellow pickled pepper at end of each skewer. Place on a platter and brush with sauce on all sides. Refrigerate for 1 hour. Grill over medium coals for 6 to 10 minutes (can also be placed under the broiler), turning once. Heat remaining sauce to boiling. Remove from heat. Stir in Equal®. Brush sauce over shrimp just before serving. Serve piping hot.

Makes 4 servings.
Calories: 150 per serving.

Robust flavor to please heartiest appetites.

Sweet and Sour Spare Ribs

1 rack spareribs (about 3 pounds)
1 recipe Sweet and Sour Sauce, (page 100)
1 tablespoon vegetable oil
2 medium onions, thinly sliced
2 medium green peppers, seeded and
  cut into thin strips
1 clove garlic, finely chopped

Ask your butcher to cut rack of spareribs into individual ribs and saw crosswise into 1½-inch pieces.

Drop ribs into 4 quarts boiling water. Lower heat and simmer 30 minutes. Drain. Dry with paper towels. Make Sweet and Sour Sauce.

Heat oil in wok or large skillet. Add onions and green peppers; stir fry 1 minute. Add spare ribs and garlic, stir-fry 1 minute. Add Sweet and Sour Sauce; cook 2 minutes or until bubbly.

Makes 20 servings, 4 pieces each.
Calories: 158 per serving.

Olé! Serve low-calorie pork rinds instead of corn chips with this south-of-the-border treat.

Taco Dip

1 pound ripe Italian plum tomatoes,
  peeled and chopped
¼ cup chopped green pepper
¼ cup sliced green onions (white and
  green parts)

7

1 large clove garlic, minced
1 tablespoon tarragon vinegar
1 tablespoon chopped basil
¼ teaspoon salt
¼ teaspoon black pepper
Few drops hot sauce
Chili powder to taste
1 packet Equal®
Low-calorie pork rinds

Combine all ingredients except Equal® and pork rinds in saucepan. Bring to a boil, lower heat, and simmer for 20 minutes. Remove from heat and add Equal®. Adjust seasonings for taste. Chill before serving. Serve dip with low-calorie crunchy pork rinds.

Makes 1½ cups.
Calories: 45 per half cup.

Delicious when spread on celery sticks or cucumber slices, and a great filling for cream puffs. The cream puff variation looks so impressive that no one can believe they're eating low-calorie tidbits.

Salmon Ball

1 can (15½ ounces) water-packed red
    salmon, drained and flaked
3 small dill pickles, chopped
1 package (4 ounces) low-calorie cream
    cheese, softened
1 tablespoon lemon juice
½ teaspoon dried dill
1 tablespoon oregano
¼ teaspoon salt

1 packet Equal®
½ cup chopped fresh parsley (optional)

Combine all ingredients except parsley in a bowl and stir to blend. Shape into a ball and chill till ready to serve. Roll ball in parsley and set on a plate.

Makes 2 cups or 32 servings, 1 tablespoon each.
Calories: 38 per serving.

Variation:
These tiny puffs are so versatile. You can fill them with crab salad, egg salad or tuna salad. Can be used for luncheon also.

Seafood-Filled Cream Puffs

Make Miniature Cream Puffs (page 94). Prepare Salmon Ball recipe, but do not refrigerate salmon or shape into ball. Split cream puffs in half and fill each with 1 tablespoon salmon mixture. Replace tops. Place a paper doily on a platter and arrange the cream puffs in the shape of a pyramid. The Salmon Ball mixture will fill 32 cream puffs. The cream puff recipe makes about 78 shells. If you are having a large crowd, double the salmon recipe, or use the leftover shells for a lovely dessert.

Makes 32 cream puffs, or 16 servings,
* 2 puffs per serving.*
Calories: 112 per serving.

A beautiful addition to any buffet. Can be used as an appetizer or entrée.

Salmon Fish Mold

1 package (8 ounces) imitation cream cheese
1 can (10½ ounces) cream of mushroom soup
2 envelopes unflavored gelatin
¼ cup water
1 can (7¾ ounces) salmon (drained and flaked)
½ cup celery
½ cup chopped green onions
1 cup diet mayonnaise, mixed with 1 packet Equal®

Garnishes:

1 green stuffed olive, cut in half
Cucumber slices
Pimiento strips
Chopped parsley
Cherry tomatoes

Combine cream cheese and soup in double boiler. Heat and stir until smooth. Dissolve gelatin in water according to package directions. Then add gelatin to soup mixture. Fold in remaining ingredients. Blend well and fold into a 5-quart mold. Chill till firm, 4 to 6 hours. Unmold and garnish as follows: Place half of olive on the eye of the fish. Overlap the cucumber slices to resemble scales along the side of the fish. Decorate the mouth, collar, and tail with pimiento strips. Sprinkle parsley along the outer rim of cucumber slices. Decorate platter with cucumber slices and cherry tomatoes. If serving mold as an appetizer, add zucchini slices or crackers for spreading.

10

Makes 6 servings for a main course.
Calories: 242 per serving.

Soups

There's a diet-wise soup in this chapter for whatever mood I'm in. Sometimes Tomato Essence appeals for its lightness. Other times, a main dish soup like Cioppino Mediterranean, with chunks of flounder, shrimp, and clams swimming in a robust broth, satisfies my appetite for heartier fare. In summer, a cup of Iced Gazpacho makes a great refresher. On chilly days, a hearty bowl of borscht provides the solace of my childhood kitchen. And when I crave a change of pace, either Tomato-Orange Soup or Summer Fruit Soup suits me perfectly.

Use soups imaginatively in menu planning. Remember that a cup of soup before a meal can diminish hunger, so that you won't reach for a second helping of the main dish. Most of the soups that follow are light and easy to prepare. The main-course soups can be made in advance, so that you need add only a salad and crusty bread to enjoy a wonderful meal on a busy day.

Soups

Delicious and rich in vitamins—especially nice on a cold winter day.

Tomato Warm-Up

2 cups tomato juice
2 teaspoons minced parsley
1 teaspoon powdered vegetable
concentrate (available in health
food stores), optional
Dash pepper
Dash mace
1 packet Equal®

Combine all ingredients except Equal® in a saucepan and heat. Remove from heat and stir in Equal®.

Makes 2 servings.
Calories: 54 per serving.

A light soup to enjoy anytime. It can be the basis for a vegetable soup—just keep a pot on hand and add leftover vegetables.

Tomato Essence

4 tomatoes, sliced
1 medium onion, sliced
1 cup mixed chopped herbs (oregano,
dill, parsley, basil)
4 tablespoons diet margarine
½ cup tomato paste
White pepper
2 cups chicken stock
1 cup skim milk
2 packets Equal®
6 tablespoons grated Parmesan cheese

12

Place tomatoes, onion, herbs, and margarine in a large pot. Cook over medium heat until onion is soft. Stir often. Add tomato paste and white pepper to taste. Purée in batches in blender or food processor until smooth. Add chicken stock. (Soup should be medium-thick.) Return to pot and heat through. Remove from heat and stir in milk and Equal®. Place soup in heat-proof bowls. Top each serving with a tablespoon of cheese.

Makes 6 servings.
Calories: 145 per serving.

A refreshingly different start for a summer meal.

Tomato-Orange Soup

3 medium tomatoes, peeled
2 small oranges
¾ cup chopped onion
2 packets instant chicken broth mix
    dissolved in 1½ cups hot water
1 cup tomato juice, chilled, mixed
    with 1 packet Equal®
½ cup dry white wine
1 tablespoon red wine vinegar
¼ teaspoon salt
¼ teaspoon pepper

Cut tomatoes and remove seeds; cut into cubes. Place in large bowl. Remove the zest of 1 orange and set aside. Remove and discard peel from both oranges. Cut oranges into cubes and add to tomatoes. Add remaining ingredients and stir to combine. Cover and chill for at least 1 hour to allow flavors to develop. Garnish with orange zest.

13

Makes 6 servings.
Calories: 70 per serving.

A sophisticated summer soup. For an attractive presentation, serve it in a cantaloupe shell.

Tropical Melon Soup

> ½ small cantaloupe, pared, seeded, and
>   cut into 1-inch chunks
> 1½ cups honeydew melon chunks
> ¼ cup fresh lemon juice
> ¼ cup fresh orange juice
> ¼ cup dry white wine
> 2 packets Equal®
> Lime zest, mixed with 2 tablespoons
>   coconut

Place melon chunks in blender or food processor and process until puréed (do this in two batches). Add juices and wine; continue processing. Stir in Equal®. Garnish with lime zest and coconut. Chill before serving.

Makes 4 servings.
Calories: 79 per serving.

This soup freezes well before the milk is added; thaw, stir in milk, and serve. If you are planning a large gathering, double the recipe and serve in a watermelon shell. It looks lovely on a buffet.

Summer Fruit Soup

> 3 cups watermelon cubes, divided into
>   2 portions
> 2 cups whole fresh strawberries,
>   divided into 2 portions
> ½ cup fresh orange juice
> 1½ teaspoons fresh lemon juice
> 1 tablespoon cornstarch
> ½ teaspoon allspice

¼ **teaspoon cinnamon**
⅛ **teaspoon ginger**
⅛ **teaspoon mace**
2 **packets Equal®**
¾ **cup skim milk**
Lemon peel for garnish

Place half of the melon in blender or food processor and purée. Add half of the strawberries and process again. Repeat with the other half. Strain fruit mixture into medium saucepan. In small cup, combine orange and lemon juices with cornstarch. Stir into fruit mixture. Add spices. Heat, stirring until mixture comes to a boil. Remove from heat, stir in Equal® and milk. Cover and chill before serving. Garnish with lemon peel.

Makes 6 servings.
Calories: 85 per serving.

This soup is great hot or cold.

Iced Gazpacho

1 **small zucchini**
1 **cucumber, diced**
½ **green pepper, diced**
½ **clove garlic, minced**
¼ **jalapeno pepper, seeded and diced**
2 **tablespoons chopped chives**
Pinch granulated garlic
1 **cup unsalted tomato juice**
¼ **cup beef bouillon**
1 **packet Equal®**

15

Place all ingredients in a blender or food processor and process for a few seconds or until the vegetables are chopped finely. Chill well. Serve in chilled soup cups.

Makes 4 servings.
Calories: 26 per serving.

A colorful summer soup, great anytime. I like to serve it from a scooped-out pumpkin shell.

Golden Carrot Soup

> 2 tablespoons diet margarine
> 8 medium carrots, pared and cut into
>   1-inch pieces
> 1 cup coarsely chopped onion
> ¼ teaspoon salt
> ¼ teaspoon pepper
> ¼ cup instant chicken bouillon
>   granules, dissolved in 3 cups
>   hot water, divided into 1 and
>   2 cups each
> ½ cup fresh orange juice
> 1 strip orange zest
> ¼ cup dry sherry
> 2 packets Equal®
> 2 tablespoons snipped chives

Heat margarine in a large heavy sauce pot until bubbly; add carrots and onion. Sauté, stirring, about 10 minutes. Stir in salt and pepper; continue to cook 1 to 2 minutes. Add 1 cup bouillon, orange juice, and strip of zest. Cover and simmer about 30 minutes, or until carrots are tender. Place carrot mixture in blender or food processor and purée in batches until all carrots are puréed. Pour purée back into sauce pot; whisk in remaining 2 cups bouillon and the sherry. Reheat, stirring, about 15 minutes. Remove from heat and stir in Equal®. Garnish with chives.

> *Makes 6 servings.*
> *Calories: 140 per serving.*

Borscht

4 pounds beef shank
1 large marrow bone
1 tablespoon salt
1 can (1 pound) tomatoes, undrained
1 medium onion, peeled and quartered
1 stalk celery, cut up
3 parsley sprigs
10 whole black peppercorns
2 bay leaves
3 cups coarsely shredded cabbage
   (1 pound)
1½ cups thickly sliced, pared carrot
   (4 medium)
1 cup chopped onion
2 tablespoons fresh dill or 3 teaspoons
   dried dill
⅓ cup cider vinegar
1 can (1 pound) julienne beets,
   undrained
1½ teaspoons salt
2 packets Equal®
Dairy sour cream
Snipped fresh dill or dried dill

Place beef, marrow bone, 1 tablespoon salt, and 2 quarts of water in an 8-quart kettle. Bring to boiling. Reduce heat; simmer covered, 1 hour. Add tomatoes, quartered onion, celery, parsley, black pepper, and bay leaves; simmer covered 2 hours. Remove from the heat. Lift out beef. Discard marrow bone. Strain soup into a colander. (There should be 9 or 10 cups.) Return soup and beef to kettle. Add cabbage, carrot, chopped onion, 2 tablespoons dill, the vinegar, beets, and 1½ teaspoons salt. Bring to boiling. Reduce heat; simmer covered 30 minutes, or until beef and vegetables are tender. Remove from heat and stir in Equal®. Refrigerate overnight. Next day, trim off fat. To serve, add a dollop of sour cream and sprinkle with dill.

17

Makes 3½ quarts, or fourteen 1-cup servings.
Calories: 71 per cup.

This steaming tureen of cioppino takes only half an hour to cook. Serve with a Greek salad and crusty bread.

Cioppino Mediterranean

¼ cup chopped green pepper
2 tablespoons finely chopped onion
1 clove garlic, minced
1 tablespoon oil
1 can (16 ounce) tomatoes, undrained,
    cut up
1 can (16 ounce) tomato sauce
½ cup dry red wine
3 tablespoons snipped parsley
½ teaspoon salt
¼ teaspoon oregano
¼ teaspoon basil
Dash pepper
1 pound frozen or fresh flounder
    fillets (thawed if frozen)
1 can shrimp (4½ ounces), drained
1 can (7½ ounces) minced clams,
    undrained
2 packets Equal®

In large saucepan, cook green pepper, onion, and garlic in oil until tender, but not brown. Add undrained tomatoes, tomato sauce, wine, parsley, salt, oregano, basil, and pepper. Bring to boiling. Reduce heat; cover and simmer 20 minutes. Cut fillets into pieces. Add flounder to broth; simmer 5 minutes. Add shrimp and undrained clams; continue simmering covered about 3 minutes more. Remove from heat and stir in Equal®.

Makes 6 servings.
Calories: 133 per serving.

Salads and
Salad Dressings

Two of the salads in this chapter hold special memories for me. Wilted Spinach Salad is a version of the first course I was served at my first meal in Chicago. It seemed so unusual then—spinach with a hot dressing that featured a hint of oriental hoisin sauce. Caesar Salad was a staple in my mother's home, and remains my favorite to this day. The crisp leaves of romaine lettuce, tossed with a mustard-spiced dressing, anchovies, and cheeses, yield a salad that can be a meal in itself. Both of these recipes defy the carrots, celery sticks, and mound of cottage cheese that is often considered the "dieter's special."

Salads can be exciting and incredibly diverse. The array I have included here is a showcase of colorful ingredients, varying textures, and contrasting tastes. Some make an excellent first course; others are designed to accompany entrées. Among the heartier salads, you'll find mouth watering California Crab Salad and Cuban Chicken Salad. These would be fine main dishes for lunch or a light supper, but they can also be arranged in small, attractive, appetizer portions. The salad dressings at the end of this chapter can be combined with all kinds of fresh vegetables, cold meats, and seafood for an infinite repertoire of low-calorie fare.

19

Garnish this refreshing aspic with Cumberland Dressing (page 31), if you wish.

Tomato-Basil Aspic

1 envelope unflavored gelatin
¼ cup cold water
1¼ cups boiling water
3 tablespoons sweet basil vinegar
⅛ teaspoon black pepper
Dash salt
2 tablespoons onion juice
4 ounces tomato paste
1 packet Equal®
Lettuce leaves
Parsley sprigs

Soften gelatin in cold water. Add boiling water and stir until gelatin is dissolved. Add vinegar, pepper, salt, onion juice, and tomato paste; blend. Add Equal® and stir again. Pour into 6 individual molds and chill. Unmold on lettuce and garnish with parsley.

Makes 6 servings.
Calories: 28 per serving.

Caesar Salad

1 recipe Caesar dressing, omitting
  Parmesan cheese (page 30)
1 large head romaine
6 anchovy fillets, drained and chopped
1 clove garlic
1 egg
¼ cup crumbled blue cheese
2 tablespoons grated Parmesan cheese
Juice of ½ lemon
3 whole anchovy fillets

Prepare dressing; refrigerate 1 hour.

Trim core from romaine. Separate into leaves, discarding wilted or discolored ones. Place in salad basket. Rinse under cold, running water; shake well to remove excess moisture. (Or wash under cold running water; drain and dry on paper towels.) Place romaine in a plastic bag; store in refrigerator until crisp and cold, several hours or overnight. Add chopped anchovies to dressing. Keep refrigerated. Rub garlic clove into the surface of a large wooden salad bowl and then discard. In a small saucepan, bring 2 inches of water to boiling. Turn off heat. Carefully lower egg into water; let stand 1 minute; then lift out. Set aside to cool. Cut the coarse ribs from large leaves of romaine. Tear in bite-size pieces into salad bowl. Shake dressing well, and pour ½ cup over romaine. Sprinkle with both kinds of cheese. Toss until all romaine is coated with salad dressing. Break egg over center of salad. Pour lemon juice directly over egg; toss well. Garnish top with the whole anchovies, if desired.

Makes 6 servings.
Calories: 111 per serving.

One of my favorites. I often serve this with an oriental dish. It also makes a nice appetizer because it can be finished at the last minute.

Wilted Spinach Salad

> 3 quarts spinach leaves, rinsed and
>   drained
> 1 cup sliced mushrooms
> 1 tablespoon plus 2 teaspoons
>   vegetable oil
> 1 tablespoon plus 1 teaspoon fresh
>   lemon juice
> 1 tablespoon plus 1 teaspoon hoisin
>   sauce
> 1 teaspoon sesame oil
> 1 packet Equal®
> 1 teaspoon sesame seeds

21

Tear spinach into bite-size pieces; combine with mushrooms. Heat vegetable oil, lemon juice, hoisin sauce, and sesame oil in large, deep skillet over medium heat, stirring constantly, until bubbly. Remove skillet from heat; stir in Equal®. Stir spinach and mushrooms into skillet; tossing until greens are slightly wilted and well-coated. Sprinkle with sesame seeds.

Makes 4 servings.
Calories: 120 per serving.

Try this low-calorie version of the original and you'll see that it makes delicious sense!

Mock Potato Salad

1 medium rutabaga
Pot of boiling water
1 packet Equal®
1 tablespoon lemon juice
1 cup minced celery with leaves
½ cup finely chopped scallions
1 medium dill pickle, chopped
1½ teaspoons salt
Dash paprika
¾ cup diet mayonnaise
2 hard-cooked eggs, chopped

Pare rutabaga and cut into 4 pieces. Drop into boiling water. Continue to boil until tender, about 30 minutes. Drain well. Cool. After rutabaga has cooled, dice (should be about 2 cups), and place in a salad bowl. Sprinkle with Equal® and lemon juice. Add celery, scallions, pickle, salt, paprika, and mayonnaise to rutabaga. Toss well. Fold in eggs. Chill before serving.

Makes 8 servings, ½ cup each.
Calories: 86 per serving.

I serve this with steak and get raves. The stuffed tomatoes look lovely on a plate.

Italian Tomato Bean Salad

> 1 recipe Tomato French dressing,
>   chilled (page 32)
> 4 medium tomatoes
> ½ cup chopped scallions
> 1 package (9 ounces) frozen Italian
>   green beans, cooked
> ½ cup chopped mushrooms
> Parsley sprigs

Prepare dressing.

Cut the tops off tomatoes and scoop out the meat inside, leaving a tomato shell. Set tops and shells aside. Place scallions, tomato meat, beans, and mushrooms in a bowl. Add ½ cup of dressing and mix well. Refrigerate covered for 1 hour to marinate. Place each tomato shell on an individual plate and divide bean mixture evenly between the 4 tomatoes. If you have any leftover, return to the refrigerator and use in salad with lettuce. Replace tomato tops and garnish with sprigs of parsley, if desired.

Makes 4 servings.
Calories: 58 per serving.

This pretty salad would enhance a special luncheon.

Cottage Cheese Lime Mold

> 1 envelope diet lime gelatin
> ½ cup mayonnaise
> ½ cup sour cream
> 1 teaspoon lemon juice
> 3 packets Equal®
> 1 pound cottage cheese (2 cups)
> ½ cantaloupe, finely diced

Salads

Prepare gelatin according to package directions, but do not add cold water. Add mayonnaise, sour cream, and lemon juice to gelatin. Beat with hand electric beater or rotary beater. Add Equal® to cottage cheese and cantaloupe. Fold cottage cheese mixture into mayonnaise mixture. Rinse 1-quart mold with cold water; shake out excess. Pour salad mixture into mold. Refrigerate for at least 2 hours before serving.

Makes 6 servings.
Calories: 177 per serving.

Keep canned beets in your pantry, and you can enjoy this salad anytime. I often make it when I am too busy to get to the grocery store.

Pickled Beet Salad

2 cups canned beets (no salt or sugar
   added), undrained
1 tablespoon red wine vinegar
1 bay leaf
1 whole clove
1 packet Equal®
Shredded lettuce
½ small onion, sliced and separated
   into rings

Drain the beet juice into a small skillet. Add the vinegar, bay leaf, and clove. Bring to a boil and simmer for 1 minute. Remove from heat and add Equal®. Let the mixture cool. Pour the cooled juice over the beets and allow to marinate overnight in the refrigerator. Lift the beets with a slotted spoon from the juice and serve on a bed of shredded lettuce. Garnish with onion rings.

24

Makes 4 servings.
Calories: 17 per serving.

Everybody has a favorite cole slaw and this is mine. It's great for picnics and barbecues.

My Favorite Cole Slaw

¼ cup Dijon mustard
¼ cup mayonnaise
½ packet Equal®
1 teaspoon lemon juice
½ teaspoon salt
1 medium cabbage, shredded (3 cups)

Mix mustard, mayonnaise, Equal®, lemon juice, and salt. Add cabbage and toss well.

Makes 6 servings, ½ cup each.
Calories: 47 per serving.

Slaw Polonaise

½ cup low-fat yogurt
¼ cup buttermilk
1 packet Equal®
Garlic powder to taste
2 tablespoons minced dill pickle
1 teaspoon poppy seed
Dash salt
Dash pepper
1 pound cabbage, shredded
Paprika

Combine all ingredients except cabbage and paprika in blender. Blend for 1 minute. Refrigerate until needed. At serving time, toss dressing with cabbage and sprinkle with paprika.

25

Makes 5 servings.
Calories: 34 per serving.

Cucumber Dill Salad

½ cup cottage cheese
2 tablespoons skim milk
½ teaspoon dried dill
½ teaspoon salt
¼ teaspoon pepper
1 tablespoon finely chopped dill
    pickle,
1 medium cucumber, thinly sliced
½ red onion, thinly sliced and
    separated into rings

Place cottage cheese and milk in blender. Blend till whipped and creamy. Add dill, salt, pepper, and dill pickle and blend till well mixed. Refrigerate until ready to use. Before serving, combine cucumber and onion slices in a bowl. Pour dressing over.

Makes 4 servings, ½ cup each.
Calories: 47 per serving.

Banana Split Salad

½ cup cottage cheese
1 large lettuce leaf
½ banana, split in half
½ cup sliced strawberries
½ cup sliced peaches
¼ cup diced pineapple
1 packet Equal®
1 tablespoon honey
¼ cup coconut
1 maraschino cherry

26

Place cottage cheese on lettuce leaf on a plate and arrange banana slices so they resemble a banana split. Set aside. Combine strawberries, peaches, and pineapple in a bowl. Add Equal® and mix. Spoon fruits onto cottage cheese.

Drizzle honey over top and sprinkle with coconut. Top with cherry.
Note: Other fruits, such as watermelon and cantaloupe, are excellent with this dish. Use whatever is in season.

Makes 1 serving.
Calories: 329.

I often serve this as a first course if the entrée is hearty. Double the recipe for luncheon entrée portions.

Asparagus with Fresh Fruit Dressing

12 large stalks asparagus, cooked and chilled
Shredded dark green lettuce
4 tablespoons chopped melon (cantaloupe or honey dew)
4 large fresh strawberries, sliced
1 small apple, finely chopped
1 teaspoon lemon juice
1 packet Equal®

Arrange asparagus on a bed of lettuce. Combine fruits, lemon juice, and Equal®. Top each salad with a fourth of the fruit mixture.

Makes 4 servings.
Calories: 26 per serving.

California Crab Salad

27

8 ounces crab meat, fresh or frozen (defrost if frozen)
½ cup sliced water chestnuts
½ cup celery, thinly sliced

¼ cup green onion, sliced
Lettuce leaves
4 stalks cooked or canned asparagus
4 artichoke hearts, canned or fresh
    cooked
2 tablespoons chopped pimiento
2 tablespoons chopped parsley
1 cup fresh bean sprouts
Capri Dressing (page 33)

Place crab, water chestnuts, celery, and onion in a dish. Mix well. Place lettuce leaves on each of 4 plates. Top with a scoop of crab salad. Place 1 asparagus stalk and 1 artichoke heart on each plate. Garnish with pimiento and parsley. Top with sprouts. Serve with Capri dressing.

Makes 4 servings.
Calories: 108 per serving, with 3
*   tablespoons dressing.*

This is a light salad that makes a delicious luncheon dish or dinner first course.

Chicken Salad À l'Orange

Orange Salad Dressing (recipe follows)
4 ounces cooked chicken, cut in strips
2 oranges, peeled and sectioned
¼ cup thinly sliced red onion
¼ cup thinly sliced celery
4 cups spinach, rinsed, and torn into
    bite-size pieces

28   Prepare Orange Salad Dressing.
    Toss together remaining ingredients. Add dressing. Toss gently so that all spinach leaves are coated.

Makes 4 servings.
Calories: 162 per serving.

Orange Salad Dressing

2 tablespoons vegetable oil
2 tablespoons white vinegar
½ teaspoon dry mustard
¼ teaspoon ground ginger
⅛ teaspoon pepper
⅛ teaspoon salt
1 packet Equal®

Place all ingredients in blender and whirl for 1 minute. Shake before serving. Keep refrigerated.

Makes about ⅓ cup.
Calories: 40 per tablespoon.

Cuban Chicken Salad

1 recipe Tomato French Dressing
   (page 32)
1 tablespoon lemon juice
1½ cups boned, cooked chicken, in
   thin strips
1 cup ripe olives, sliced
⅓ cup green pepper, cut into strips
¼ cup red onion, finely chopped
2 to 3 tablespoons pimiento, in thin strips
1 avocado, cut into crescents
4 cups shredded lettuce

Prepare dressing and add lemon juice. Refrigerate until ready to use. Combine all salad ingredients except avocado. Refrigerate. Just before serving, add avocado. Arrange salad on bed of shredded lettuce. Shake dressing and pour over salad.

29

Makes 4 servings.
Calories: 278 per serving without dressing;
   308 with dressing.

Parmesan Caesar Dressing

4 tablespoons tarragon vinegar
6 tablespoons safflower oil
2 tablespoons olive oil
1 teaspoon lemon juice
2 teaspoons Dijon mustard
1 tablespoon grated Parmesan cheese
1 teaspoon seasoned salt
¼ teaspoon garlic powder
¼ teaspoon dry mustard
½ packet Equal®
1 egg

Place all ingredients in blender. Blend for 30 seconds. Refrigerate. Dressing is best when used within 1 week.

Makes 1½ cups.
Calories: 37 per tablespoon.

Two low-calorie versions of old standbys.

Thousand Island Dressing

¾ cup cottage cheese, whipped in
   blender with 2 tablespoons skim
   milk
½ cup tomato juice
1 tablespoon chopped dill pickle
2 teaspoons onion flakes
2 teaspoons minced green pepper
2 packets Equal®

30

Place all ingredients in blender and whirl for 1 minute. Cover and refrigerate until ready to use.

Makes 1½ cups.
Calories: 6 per tablespoon.

Russian Dressing

⅓ cup low-calorie mayonnaise
1⅓ cups cottage cheese,
   whipped in blender with 2
   tablespoons skim milk
⅓ cup tomato juice
1 tablespoon lemon juice
2 tablespoons onion flakes
1 tablespoon chopped parsley
Drop of hot sauce

Place all ingredients in blender and whirl for 1 minute. Cover and refrigerate until ready to use.

Makes 1 cup.
Calories: 31 per tablespoon.

Cumberland Dressing

1 bottle (12 ounces) low-calorie
   ketchup (no sugar or salt added)
1 cup pure apple juice
½ cup red wine vinegar
Juice of 1 lemon, strained
1 teaspoon dry mustard
Coarsely ground black pepper
1 packet Equal®
2 stalks celery, finely chopped
1 cucumber, pared
1 green or red sweet pepper, chopped
Tops of 2 green onions

Blend all the ingredients except the vegetables, being careful to dissolve the mustard so there will be no lumps. Fold the vegetables in just before serving to preserve the freshness.

Makes 2 cups.
Calories: 10 to 15 per tablespoon.

31

Great for cole slaw or cucumber salad.

Creamy Yogurt Dressing

1 cup (8 ounces) plain yogurt
¼ cup chopped green onion
2 tablespoons Parmesan cheese
½ packet Equal®
½ teaspoon salt
¼ teaspoon dried dill

Combine all ingredients in blender and process at medium speed until smooth. Store in refrigerator. Dressing is best when used within 1 week.
Note: Dressing may be used as a dip for celery, carrot sticks, and other fresh vegetables.

Makes 1¼ cups.
Calories: 9 per tablespoon.

Good on any green salad or as a marinade for meat.

Tomato French Dressing

1½ cups tomato juice
¾ cup vinegar
1 teaspoon Worcestershire sauce
1 teaspoon salt
1 teaspoon dry mustard
¼ teaspoon pepper
⅛ teaspoon garlic powder
3 packets Equal®

32

In a saucepan, combine all ingredients except Equal®. Cook over medium heat until mixture is reduced to about 1 cup. Remove from heat and stir in Equal®. Chill.

Makes 1¼ cups.
Calories: 6 per tablespoon.

Good with fish salads, this dressing can also be served warm over fish.

Capri Dressing

> ½ cup cottage cheese, whipped in
>   blender
> 2 tablespoons horseradish
> 1 tablespoon low-calorie mayonnaise
> 1 tablespoon lemon juice
> 1 teaspoon Worcestershire sauce
> ½ teaspoon dry mustard
> 2 packets Equal®
> 2 tablespoons parsley

Place all ingredients except parsley in blender and whirl for 1 minute. Mix in parsley and refrigerate until ready to use.

Makes 2½ cups.
Calories: 5 per tablespoon.

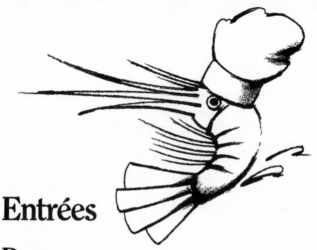

Entrées

People and places that have meant a great deal to me are reflected in many of the entrées I love to prepare. When I recall the festive family celebrations of my childhood, the fondest food memory is of roast leg of lamb, cooked until the meat reached a delicate pink—never medium or (perish the thought!) well done. The pungent aroma of garlic filled the house and signaled the beginning of a great feast.

In New Orleans, I was introduced to Creole cooking in a tiny bistro just off Bourbon Street. There, the cook, Jenna, showed me how shrimp can reign supreme, in her Creole Jambalaya. (I hope Jenna will forgive me for the small changes I've made in her recipe for the sake of our waistlines—something she didn't give a hoot about!)

On the East Coast, I discovered Grecian Chicken, notable for its lemon-butter sauce accented with oregano and garlic, at a New York restaurant. Contrast this with the Canton Chicken Wings, laced with sherry and honey, served in a quaint restaurant in Chinatown. In New Jersey, we found a charming restaurant in an out-of-the-way spot. It wasn't at all fancy—you brought your own wine and walked in without reservations. But the meal always featured a wonderful dish of pasta, sometimes smothered under a blanket of whole clams in a delightful garlic-butter sauce, and other times covered with an herb-fragrant fresh tomato sauce.

Each time I travel to California, I look forward to my favorite seafood restaurant in San Francisco. Imagine eating salmon that was pulled from the sea only twenty-four hours before, poached in a delicate sweet and sour sauce.

I hope the recipes for these dishes and the many others in this chapter signal a sensible and promising change in your

35

cooking and eating habits. The entrées I have included represent many of the ways in which we have become a health-conscious nation. Meat does not play the dominant role it once did; nowadays, servings are smaller and we add more vegetable accompaniments. Fish and chicken offer change-of-pace flavors and fewer calories. Pasta remains a passion— but in weight-wary quantities. And because main dish soups and salads present nutritious alternatives to meat-and-potato meal plans, I've included many additional entrées in the Soups and Salads chapters.

A great southern favorite. A salad and a fruit dessert turn it into a complete meal.

Creole Jambalaya

2 tablespoons diet margarine
1 cup diced cooked ham
½ cup chopped green pepper
½ cup chopped onion
1 garlic clove, minced
1 can (10¾ ounces) condensed tomato
    soup
⅓ cup water
1 medium bay leaf, crushed
¼ teaspoon crushed oregano
¼ teaspoon salt
Dash pepper
1 can (6¾ ounces) shrimp, drained
2 packets Equal®
1½ cups cooked rice

36   Melt margarine in large skillet. Stir in ham, green pepper, onion, and garlic. Add soup, water, bay leaf, oregano, salt, and pepper. Cook over medium-high heat 20 minutes. Add shrimp; cook until heated through, 2 to 3 minutes. Remove from heat; stir in Equal®. Serve over rice.

Makes 4 servings.
Calories: 252 per serving.

Tip: To prepare in microwave oven, place ham, green pepper, onion, garlic and margarine in a 3-quart casserole. Place in microwave oven and microwave at HIGH 5 to 6 minutes or until vegetables are tender. Stir in soup, water, shrimp, and seasonings. Continue cooking in microwave oven at HIGH 4 minutes. Remove from microwave, stir in Equal®. Serve over cooked rice.

This dish is wonderful served with plain white rice and a salad.

Shrimp Louisiana

Sauce:

> 1 can (15 ounces) tomato purée
> ½ cup water
> 3 tablespoons white vinegar
> 3 tablespoons Worcestershire sauce
> 2 tablespoons orange juice concentrate, thawed
> 1 tablespoon prepared mustard
> ¼ teaspoon hot sauce
> ½ teaspoon garlic powder
> ¼ teaspoon salt
> 3 packets Equal®
> 12 ounces cooked shrimp

In a saucepan combine all sauce ingredients except Equal®. Slowly bring to a boil, stirring constantly. Remove from heat. Stir in Equal®. Add shrimp to sauce and serve. Sauce yield: 2½ cups.

Makes 4 servings of shrimp and sauce.
Calories: 171 per serving.

37

Hawaiian Baked Fish

1½ cups packaged pre-cooked
  (Minute) rice
1 pound fresh (or thawed frozen)
  flounder fillets
2 tablespoons diet margarine
1 tablespoon instant minced onion
1 tablespoon diced pimiento
1 teaspoon salt
1 teaspoon parsley flakes
½ teaspoon curry powder (optional)
1¼ cups pineapple juice
2 tablespoons lemon juice
3 packets Equal®

Cook rice according to package directions and place in heat-proof serving dish. Place fish in baking dish; dot with margarine. Bake in preheated 325° oven 25 minutes; remove fish with spatula and place over rice. Keep warm in low oven while preparing sauce.

Combine minced onion, pimiento, salt, parsley, curry powder, pineapple juice, and lemon juice in saucepan; cover and heat to boiling. Remove from heat; stir in Equal®. Spoon sauce over fish and rice.

Makes 4 servings.
Calories: 166 per serving.

Tip: Other mild-flavored fish such as turbot or monkfish can be used.

To prepare in microwave oven, combine rice, minced onion, pimiento, salt, parsley, curry powder, pineapple and lemon juices, and Equal® in 8-inch square baking dish. Arrange fish over rice mixture. Dot margarine over top. Cover dish with plastic wrap, punching 2 or 3 holes in top for venting. Place dish in microwave oven. Cook at HIGH 10 or 12 minutes, giving dish ½ turn after 5 minutes. Remove from oven and let stand covered about 2 minutes before serving.

An unusual, fast-cooking treat.

Salmon Primavera

1 can (7¾ ounce) salmon
1 clove garlic, minced
½ cup green onions, sliced into ½-inch
   pieces
⅓ cup diet margarine
1 pound fresh broccoli, trimmed and
   split into flowerets
2 cups thinly sliced zucchini
2 teaspoons basil leaves
1 cup sliced mushrooms
1 cup cherry tomatoes, halved
½ cup soy sauce
1 tablespoon cornstarch
2 packets Equal®

Drain salmon and break into chunks; set aside. In wok
or large skillet, cook garlic and onions in margarine over
medium-high heat for 1 minute. Add broccoli, zucchini, and
basil. Cook for about 2 minutes. Add the mushrooms and
cook for 2 more minutes. Test broccoli for doneness. Add
tomatoes and cook for 1 minute. Meanwhile, mix soy sauce,
cornstarch, and Equal® in a cup till Equal® is dissolved. Add
salmon to vegetables and cook for 1 minute. Pour sauce
over vegetables and stir once. Remove from heat and serve
immediately.

Makes 4 servings.
Calories: 318 per serving.

Entrées

Simple and delicious.

Sweet and Sour Salmon

1 cup water
¼ cup red wine vinegar
1 shallot, chopped
1 tablespoon pickling spice
1 teaspoon cracked peppercorn
5 salmon steaks (3 ounces each)
1 packet Equal®

Mix all ingredients except salmon and Equal®. Marinate salmon for 2 to 3 hours in the mixture. Drain marinade into a small shallow pan or skillet; heat marinade to a simmer. Use a spatula to place the salmon steaks into the hot liquid. Cover lightly with foil. Cook salmon until it is opaque and flakes. Remove salmon to platter. Add Equal® to sauce and garnish each steak with 1 tablespoon of poaching liquid.

Makes 5 servings.
Calories: 146 per serving.

For a delectable Oriental meal, serve with fried rice and stir-fried vegetables.

Canton Chicken Wings

1 pound chicken wings
2 tablespoons diet oil
4 tablespoons soy sauce
3 tablespoons sherry wine
1 teaspoon vinegar
2 tablespoons honey
2 scallions (green and white parts),
    minced
1 large clove garlic, minced
1 teaspoon grated fresh ginger

1/4 teaspoon cayenne pepper (or to taste)
4 packets Equal®

Wipe wings with a damp cloth; pat dry. Cut them through the joints into 3 pieces each. Discard the wing tips, or use them to make chicken broth. Heat oil in skillet or wok and sauté chicken pieces until nicely browned on both sides, about 4 to 5 minutes. Blend soy sauce, sherry, vinegar, and honey; add soy sauce mixture and all other ingredients except Equal® to the skillet. Cover tightly and simmer gently for about half an hour or until chicken is tender. Stir a few times while cooking. Remove from heat and place chicken pieces on a platter. Stir in Equal® and coat chicken pieces with sauce.

Makes 4 servings.
Calories: 167 per serving.

Tantalizing herb flavor. It goes well with green beans and Wilted Spinach Salad.

Grecian Chicken

1 frying chicken (2 to 2½ pounds),
   cut up
3 tablespoons oregano
1 teaspoon garlic powder
1/4 teaspoon salt
1/4 teaspoon pepper
1 tablespoon diet margarine
1 cup lemon juice
1 cup white table wine
1 teaspoon Worcestershire sauce
1/4 teaspoon garlic powder
2 tablespoons cornstarch
1/4 cup water
3 packets Equal®

41

Sprinkle chicken pieces with oregano, 1 teaspoon garlic powder, salt, and pepper. Place chicken skin side up in a non-stick shallow casserole. Melt margarine; brush chicken pieces. Bake at 375° for 40 minutes. Combine lemon juice, wine, Worcestershire sauce, and ¼ teaspoon garlic powder; pour over chicken. Cover and bake 20 minutes or until tender. Remove chicken. Combine cornstarch and water; add to pan juices. Cook over medium heat, stirring constantly until thickened. Remove from heat; stir in Equal®. Serve sauce over chicken.

Makes 4 servings.
Calories: 365 per serving.

I like to round out a meal of this Italian classic with soup and a salad.

Chicken Cacciatore

4 chicken breasts (3½ ounces each)
4 medium tomatoes, peeled and
   chopped
1 medium onion, sliced
1 tablespoon oregano
1 tablespoon rosemary
1 tablespoon basil
1 clove garlic, minced
2 ounces dietetic ketchup
1 packet Equal®

Trim the chicken of all excess fat. Brown in oven at 500° for 15 minutes. Combine remaining ingredients except Equal® and pour over chicken. Return chicken to oven and bake covered at 350° for 30 minutes. Remove the chicken from the sauce; stir in Equal®. Pour sauce over chicken and serve.

42

Makes 4 servings.
Calories: 146 per serving.

Pork in Orange Sauce

> 1 tablespoon finely shredded orange
>   peel
> ½ cup orange juice
> 2 tablespoons soy sauce
> 2 teaspoons cornstarch
> ⅛ teaspoon ground ginger
> 2 large carrots, thinly sliced
> 2 stalks celery, chopped (1 cup)
> 2 tablespoons vegetable cooking oil
> 1 pound lean boneless pork, cut into
>   ½-inch cubes
> 8 medium cashews
> 1 packet Equal®

Combine orange peel, orange juice, soy sauce, cornstarch, and ginger; set aside. In wok or skillet, stir fry carrots and celery in hot oil about 4 minutes or till crisp-tender. Remove from wok and set aside. Stir fry pork 4 to 5 minutes or until browned. (Add more oil if necessary.) Add orange juice mixture and cashews. Cook and stir till thickened and bubbly. Add Equal® and then vegetables to wok. Cover and heat through 1 minute.

> *Makes 6 servings.*
> *Calories: 259 per serving.*

Perfect for a large family celebration.

Roast Leg of Lamb with Mint Sauce

> 1 leg of lamb (7 to 8 pounds)
> White pepper
> 3 or 4 cloves garlic, sliced
> Dried rosemary

43

Mint Sauce:

> **For 5 servings sauce, ¼ cup each:**
> **1 cup unsweetened pineapple juice**
> **3 tablespoons red wine vinegar**
> **Fresh mint leaves, chopped fine**
> **3 packets Equal®**

Trim off all visible fat from lamb. Season with white pepper and insert garlic slices by making slits in meat. Sprinkle with rosemary. Roast at 400° until medium rare. This usually works out to 20 to 25 minutes per pound. You will need to check your oven temperature to guarantee the degree of doneness that you like. Allow the roast to rest so that by serving time it should be medium. Combine pineapple juice, vinegar, and mint leaves; heat through. Add Equal® to the sauce before serving. Serve on the side in small dip cups. Serve 2 ounces of thin-sliced lamb per person.

Calories: 146 per serving with sauce.

Tip: Sauce can also be served with lamb chops.

Wok Steak

> **1 recipe Sweet and Sour Sauce,**
> **(page 100)**
> **2 tablespoons diet oil**
> **1 medium onion, sliced**
> **1 large zucchini, sliced into half-dollar**
> **slices**
> **½ pound pea pods**
> **½ pound mushrooms, sliced**
> **½ can (8 ounce size) water chestnuts,**
> **sliced**
> **1 pound beef fillet or London broil,**
> **thinly sliced**
> **2 tablespoons sesame seeds**

Prepare Sweet and Sour Sauce; set aside. In a wok or skillet, heat 2 tablespoons oil. Add vegetables in order of listing, allowing 1 minute cooking time between each addition. Move vegetables to one side of wok and place steak in oil. Cook about 1 minute and turn; cook 1 minute more. Toss steak with vegetables. Add Sweet and Sour Sauce and sesame seeds. Heat for 1 minute. Serve immediately.

Makes 6 servings.
Calories: 275 per serving.

A low-calorie version of a traditional dish.

Stuffed Bell Peppers

4 small green peppers
½ pound lean ground beef
Dash white pepper
1 cup unsalted whole tomatoes,
    chopped and mixed with 1 packet
    of Equal®
¼ cup small yellow onion, chopped
¾ cup unsalted defatted beef broth
1 packet Equal®

Wash the green peppers and remove the seeds. Set aside. Brown the ground beef in a dry, hot pan and season with pepper. Drain off all the fat. Set aside. Combine half the chopped tomatoes and all the chopped onion. Simmer for a few minutes. Combine the ground meat and the tomato-onion mixture; spoon mixture into peppers. Place the peppers in a shallow pan and pour the remaining tomatoes and the beef broth around the peppers. Cover the pan with aluminum foil and bake for 45 to 50 minutes in a preheated 350° oven. Cool slightly before serving. Reduce the liquid in the pan by half; add the Equal®. Glaze each pepper with a little sauce before serving.

45

Makes 2 servings.
Calories: 262 per serving.

Stuffed Eggplant Rolls

1 medium eggplant (about 1¼ pounds)
1 egg
½ cup skim milk
2 tablespoons vegetable oil
1 cup dried bread crumbs

Filling:
12 ounces cottage cheese
½ cup parsley leaves
Oregano leaves

Sauce:
1 can (15 ounces) tomato sauce
1 cup water
2 tablespoons oregano
2 tablespoons parsley
1 teaspoon garlic powder
¼ teaspoon pepper
2 packets Equal®
2 tablespoons grated Parmesan cheese

About 40 minutes before serving, preheat broiler. Spray
15½ x 10½ inch jelly-roll pan with vegetable spray lightly
in an up-and-down motion. Cut eggplant lengthwise into
twelve ⅛-inch slices. In pie plate with fork, mix egg, milk,
and oil. Place bread crumbs on waxed paper. Dip eggplant
slices in egg mixture, then coat with bread crumbs.
Arrange slices in jelly-roll pan in 1 layer; broil 5 to 7 minutes
until tender and lightly browned.

Meanwhile, as eggplant is broiling, prepare filling. In a
medium bowl, mix cottage cheese, parsley, and oregano.
Remove eggplant from oven and set aside. Adjust oven temperature to 400°. Starting along narrow end of eggplant
slice, evenly spoon about 2 rounded tablespoons of the filling in a ½-inch wide strip; roll eggplant jelly-roll fashion.
Repeat with remaining eggplant slices.

Place eggplant rolls, seam side down, in 12 x 8-inch baking dish. Return to oven and bake 10 to 15 minutes or until
heated through. While eggplant is baking, prepare sauce. In
medium saucepan, add all sauce ingredients except Equal®
and Parmesan. Bring to a boil. Remove from heat and stir in

Equal®. Remove eggplant from oven and place rolls on a platter. Cover with sauce and sprinkle with Parmesan.

Makes 6 servings, 2 rolls each.
Calories: 189 per serving.

Pasta served any way is one of my favorite meals. These recipes will make you forget you're dieting.

Pasta with Red Clam Sauce or Tomato Basil Sauce

Red Clam Sauce or Tomato Basil Sauce
(recipes follow).
1 package spaghetti (12 ounces)
4 quarts boiling water
Salt to taste (optional)

Prepare either sauce.

Add spaghetti to the boiling water. Add salt, if using, and stir vigorously until water begins to boil again, approximately 30 seconds. Cook 8 to 12 minutes. Drain. Add sauce and serve.

Makes 6 servings pasta, 2 ounces each.
Calories: 210, without sauce.

Red Clam Sauce

4 cans clams (10½ ounces each)
2 tablespoons oil
1 cup finely chopped onion
3 cloves garlic, minced
3 cups drained tomatoes (three 8-ounce cans)
4 cans (8 ounces each) tomato sauce
2 teaspoons salt

47

½ teaspoon oregano
¼ teaspoon pepper
1 packet Equal®
Grated Parmesan cheese

Drain clams, reserving 1½ cups of the liquor. Heat oil in a large saucepan. Add onion and garlic and sauté until lightly browned. Add clams, clam liquor, tomatoes, tomato sauce, salt, oregano, and pepper. Mix well. Cook over low heat uncovered about 25 minutes. Remove from heat and stir in Equal®. Serve over spaghetti with grated cheese.

Makes about 5 cups, or enough for 10 to 12 servings.
Calories: 103 per serving.

Tomato Basil Sauce

2 pounds ripe Italian plum tomatoes or any from your garden, peeled and chopped
½ cup sliced green onions
½ cup sliced mushrooms
3 cloves garlic, finely chopped
⅔ teaspoon salt
¼ teaspoon coarse black pepper
2 tablespoons tarragon vinegar
¼ cup dried crushed basil leaves or 1 cup firmly packed fresh basil leaves
1 packet Equal®

Combine tomatoes, green onions, mushrooms, garlic, salt, pepper, vinegar and basil in bowl. Toss to mix well. Cover tightly. Set aside at room temperature 2 hours so flavors can blend. If using for pasta sauce, heat to desired temperature, remove sauce from heat, and stir in Equal®. If you are using as a salad dressing or dip, add Equal® and stir before serving.

Makes 3 cups, or enough sauce for 1 pound of pasta.
Calories: 57 per ½ cup.

Vegetables

The bold colors and varied shapes of vegetables always remind me of the time, long ago, when I first began to paint. My French grandmother always had a garden assortment on hand, and it provided excellent subjects for a novice artist. Vegetables made the best models, because they could maintain a pose for hours and assume any position I wanted! Moreover, the deep purple of an eggplant, plump and ripe, next to a white cauliflower, highlighted by a golden bunch of carrots, framed with lacy leaves, provided a striking subject.

As I began to cook vegetables, as well as paint them, I learned that you must understand your materials. Begin by tasting vegetables raw and noting the color and feel of the texture. Then continue tasting as they cook, and recognize how easily both the color and texture can be destroyed by heat. It is only recently that Americans have discovered how much better vegetables taste raw or cooked so little that they remain somewhat crisp, as in stir-fried Chinese and Japanese dishes. Some crisp-cooked vegetables, such as asparagus and cauliflower, have so much natural flavor that a little margarine is all the added seasoning they need. Other vegetables are enhanced by a touch of sweetness or a light sauce, and it's these I've concentrated on in this chapter.

Sweet and Sour Stir-Fry

1 recipe Sweet and Sour Sauce
   (page 100)
1 tablespoon vegetable oil
3 carrots, sliced on a diagonal
2 stalks celery, sliced on a diagonal
1 medium onion, quartered and
   separated
½ head red cabbage, shredded
½ head green cabbage, shredded
2 medium zucchini, sliced
½ cup water chestnuts, sliced
¼ cup pimiento, chopped

Make sauce first and keep warm.

Heat wok or frying pan to medium to high heat. Add 1 tablespoon vegetable oil. Stir together carrots, celery, and onion. Cook for about 2 minutes. Add cabbage, zucchini, and water chestnuts. Cook for about 2 more minutes. If vegetables seem to be sticking, add ¼ cup of water and turn heat down to medium. Cover and cook for 1 minute. Uncover and add pimiento. Stir and remove from heat. Place vegetables in a bowl and stir in sauce. Serve at once.

Makes 6 servings.
Calories: 62 per serving.

Served right in the shell, spaghetti squash is a dazzling accompaniment for roast chicken or turkey.

Golden Spaghetti Squash

1 spaghetti squash (2½ to 3 pounds)
2 tablespoons diet margarine at room
   temperature
2 packets Equal®
¼ teaspoon ground cinnamon

Dash salt
1 orange, peeled and chopped

Preheat oven to 375°. Cut squash in half lengthwise. Using
a spoon, scrape out seeds and loose stringy portion. Place
squash halves, cut side down, on a shallow baking pan.
Bake 35 to 45 minutes, or until tender. While baking squash,
combine in a bowl margarine, Equal®, cinnamon, and salt.
Invert baked squash halves. Using a fork, pull spaghetti-like
strands up. Add half the margarine mixture to each cooked
squash half. Lightly toss with fork. Top with orange pieces.
Serve warm.

Makes 6 servings.
Calories: 72 per serving.

This dish tastes even better when made ahead and reheated.
It makes an excellent cold dip for vegetables, too.

Ratatouille

½ **small red onion, thinly sliced**
½ **small green pepper, sliced**
1 **clove garlic, minced**
1 **can (16 ounces) whole tomatoes,**
    coarsely chopped
1 **cup bite-sized zucchini chunks**
1 **eggplant, pared and cut into**
    ½-**inch cubes**
1½ **teaspoons oregano**
1½ **teaspoons chopped parsley**
Black pepper
1 **teaspoon salt**
1 **packet Equal®**

51

In a heavy saucepan, mix the onion, green pepper, garlic,
and tomatoes. Add zucchini, eggplant, oregano, parsley,
pepper, and salt. Toss together. Bring mixture to a boil and
simmer until fork tender. Remove from the heat and stir
in Equal®. Adjust the seasonings as desired. This dish is bet-

ter when held and reheated. If you are not going to serve right away, do not add Equal® until you have reheated and then add the Equal® before serving. Leftovers are excellent served as a low-calorie dip for veggies.

Makes 5 servings.
Calories: 17 per serving.

These special beans go extremely well with baked fish.

Swedish Green Beans in Mustard Sauce

2 packages (9 ounces each) frozen
   whole green beans

Sauce: 3 tablespoons diet margarine
3 tablespoons flour
1 teaspoon dry mustard
1 tablespoon chopped fresh dill or
   1 teaspoon dried dill
½ teaspoon salt
Pinch pepper
¾ cup skim milk
3 tablespoons prepared mustard
1 egg yolk, slightly beaten with
   1 tablespoon cider vinegar
1 packet Equal®

Cook beans; drain and place in a saucepan. Prepare sauce: Melt margarine in a small saucepan over moderate heat. Blend in flour, dry mustard, dill, salt, and pepper; cook 1 minute. Add milk, stirring until thickened and smooth, 2 or 3 minutes. Blend in prepared mustard. Mix a little hot sauce into egg yolk mixture; stir back into saucepan. Turn down heat to lowest point and add beans. Keep stirring until heated through, about 3 minutes. Remove from heat and stir in Equal®.

Makes 6 servings.
Calories: 81 per serving.

I often serve this with roast duck or chicken because they can be put in the oven.

Baked Acorn or Hubbard Squash

2 small acorn or hubbard squash
1 cup orange juice
1 teaspoon cinnamon and 1 teaspoon
   nutmeg mixed together
2 packets Equal®

Cut squash into fourths and remove the seeds. Braise the squash covered in a shallow pan until somewhat softened, about 10 to 15 minutes. Sprinkle with orange juice and cinnamon and nutmeg mixture. Bake the squash uncovered in the oven at 350° for about 20 to 25 minutes or until a fork can pierce the squash easily. Remove from oven and sprinkle with Equal®. Stir the center with a spoon and serve immediately.

Makes 4 servings.
Calories: 51 per serving.

You can be ready for company any time with this recipe if you keep canned beets in the pantry.

Hot Spiced Beets

2 cups fresh or canned dietetic beets,
   sliced
½ cup water
2 cloves
1 bay leaf
1 tablespoon red wine vinegar
1 packet Equal®

Drain the juice from the beets, if using canned. Add ½ cup water to saucepan and bring to a boil with the cloves and

Vegetables

bay leaf. Add the vinegar (and beets, if using fresh). Heat
10 minutes. Remove the cloves and bay leaf. If using canned
beets, add the beets to the hot liquid and heat through
for about 1 minute. Remove from heat and stir in Equal®.
Serve hot.

Makes 4 servings.
Calories: 37 per serving.

Serve this dish with leg of lamb for an elegant spring dinner.

Baby Carrots à l'Orange

1½ cups unsalted chicken broth
20 baby carrots or 2 large carrots,
   pared and sliced
1 medium onion, chopped
1 small orange, peeled and diced
1½ packets Equal®

Heat the chicken broth to boiling. Add the carrots and
onion; cover and cook until nearly tender, approximately
7 to 8 minutes. Add the orange and cook 4 to 5 minutes more.
Remove from heat and stir in Equal®. Serve hot.

Makes 4 servings.
Calories: 37 per serving.

Breakfast Treats

Nowadays my ideal day begins in my small patio garden, listening to the birds chirping and gazing at the butter flies flitting from flower to flower. I've set the table with pink and white checked place mats and placed a basket of petunias in the center. On a tray I have placed a steaming pot of coffee, orange marmalade, and some toast to munch slowly. I consider breakfast very important and believe that everyone, dieting or not, should make this the most important meal of the day. It is a wonderful time to contemplate your plans for the day, and share a special time with your loved ones.

Whenever we consider breakfast, eggs always come to mind, and with good reason. Eggs are versatile; whether boiled, poached, or scrambled just so, they are delicious and satisfying. Cottage cheese, cream cheese and fruit combine well with eggs to yield low-calorie breakfast treats.

The possibilities in this chapter range from a blintz omelet made in minutes to a Swedish pancake for the times you can afford to linger over brunch. You'll also find tantalizing variations on fruit and toast here; for marmalade, jelly, and jam, see the recipes listed in the Index. And don't overlook some of the terrific shakes for breakfast in the Beverages chapter. These can be made in seconds, so that you needn't miss the most important meal even on busiest days.

55

Breakfast Treats

These are both quick and easy to make.

Spiced Grapefruit

> 1 medium grapefruit
> 2 tablespoons CinnSweet® (see
>   note below)

Split grapefruit into two portions; sprinkle with
CinnSweet®.

> *Makes 2 servings.*
> *Calories: 48 per serving.*

Cinnamon Toast

> 2 pieces of diet bread
> 2 tablespoons diet margarine
> 2 tablespoons CinnSweet® (see
>   note below)

Toast bread and spread with margarine. Sprinkle
CinnSweet® on top.

> *Makes 1 serving (2 slices).*
> *Calories: 90.*

Note: CinnSweet® is a mixture of cinnamon and Equal®.
Equal® combines beautifully with cinnamon in a proportion
of 2 teaspoons cinnamon to 6 packets Equal®. I always
keep a jar on hand because it is used in many recipes in this
book.

French Toast

> **1 tablespoon diet margarine**
> **1 egg, slightly beaten**
> **¼ cup skim milk**
> **½ teaspoon vanilla**
> **Dash salt**
> **6 slices of diet bread**
> **CinnSweet® (see page 56)**

Heat margarine in a heavy skillet. Place the egg, milk, vanilla, and salt into a bowl; blend with a fork. Dip bread into egg mixture and sauté in margarine on both sides to a golden brown. Sprinkle each side with CinnSweet®.

> *Makes 6 servings.*
> *Calories: 64 per serving.*

This omelet recalls the taste of high-calorie blintzes and makes a great brunch choice.

Blintz Omelet

> **8 eggs**
> **½ cup creamed cottage cheese**
> **½ cup low-calorie cream cheese,**
> **   softened**
> **2 packets Equal®**
> **1 teaspoon vanilla**
> **½ teaspoon cinnamon**
> **Pinch of salt**
> **¼ cup skim milk**
> **2 tablespoons diet margarine**
> **2 tablespoons sour cream**

57

Combine all ingredients except margarine and sour cream in blender. Blend until smooth. Melt margarine in a large omelet pan. Pour egg mixture into omelet pan and tilt the pan to spread mixture to the edges. Cook over low heat until eggs begin to set. Loosen eggs from sides of pan with a spatula. Tilt the pan again to allow uncooked egg mixture to spread to the sides. When center is firm, carefully fold 2 of the outer edges of the omelet into the center. Garnish with sour cream.

Makes 4 servings.
Calories: 265 per serving.

In summer I vary this recipe according to the best fruit available—peaches, nectarines, or fresh berries.

Creamy Peach Omelet

> 1 package (8 ounces) low-calorie cream
> cheese, softened
> 8 eggs
> Pinch of salt
> ¼ cup heavy cream
> 2 packets Equal®
> 2 tablespoons diet margarine
> ½ cup peaches mixed in blender with
> 2 packets Equal®

Combine all ingredients except margarine and peaches in a bowl. Beat till smooth. Melt margarine in omelet pan; pour in egg mixture. Cook over low heat until the eggs begin to set. Loosen eggs with a spatula from the sides of the pan. Tilt pan to allow uncooked egg mixture to spread to the sides. When center is firm, spoon peaches into the center of the omelet. Carefully fold 2 of the outer edges of the omelet into the center.

58

Makes 4 servings.
Calories: 311 per serving.

Takes a little time, but it's worth it.

Swedish Peach Pancake

Batter: **4 eggs**
½ cup skim milk
2 tablespoons diet margarine, melted
1 teaspoon vanilla
½ cup all-purpose flour
½ teaspoon baking powder
¼ teaspoon cinnamon
Dash of salt

Filling: **2 tablespoons diet margarine**
**1 large fresh peach or two small
    peaches, peeled and sliced
    ¼ inch thick**
½ teaspoon cinnamon

Glaze: **8 packets Equal®**
½ teaspoon cinnamon
3 tablespoons boiling water

Mix batter ingredients together in blender. Mix well until smooth. Let rest 30 minutes. While batter is resting, prepare filling. Melt margarine in a 10-inch oven-proof skillet. Add peach slices. Sprinkle slices with cinnamon and toss over low heat for 3 minutes. Pour batter over peaches and bake in preheated 425° oven for 15 minutes. Reduce heat to 350° for additional 15 minutes. Remove from oven. Blend glaze ingredients and drizzle over top of pancake. Cut into 4 wedges to serve.

Makes 4 servings.
Calories: 229 per serving.

Tip: 1 apple, pared and thinly sliced, or 1 cup sliced strawberries can also be used.

Very French and very elegant for brunch.

French Fruit and Cream Cheese Crêpes

Batter: **2 eggs**
¼ cup skim milk
2 tablespoons water
4 tablespoons all-purpose flour
⅛ teaspoon salt

Filling: **3 ounces low-calorie cream cheese**
6 tablespoons dry curd cottage cheese
1 egg
4 packets Equal®

Strawberry Sauce:
2 cups fresh strawberries
1 tablespoon lemon juice
6 packets Equal®

Batter: Place eggs, milk, and water in a bowl. Beat well, and add the flour and salt. Beat again until smooth. Spray a crêpe pan with vegetable spray and heat pan over medium heat. When pan is hot, spoon 2 tablespoons of batter into pan and rotate the pan to spread evenly. Crêpe is ready when the edges are browned. Turn crêpe onto plate and fill.
Filling: Place all ingredients in blender. Blend until smooth. Spread filling on crêpe and roll up jelly-roll style. Dust with Equal® or top with Strawberry Sauce.
Sauce: Blend all ingredients in blender and spoon over crêpes.

Makes 6 servings, 2 crêpes each.
Calories: 122 per serving, with strawberry
sauce.

60

Tip: Other fruits such as blueberries, peaches, or pineapple can be used for the sauce.

A family favorite. Serve with homemade jam.

Blueberry Muffins

1½ cups all-purpose flour
2 teaspoons baking powder
½ teaspoon salt
½ teaspoon vanilla
2 eggs
½ cup skim milk
2 tablespoons diet oil
1 cup frozen blueberries, thawed and
   juice reserved
3 tablespoons hot skim milk
10 packets Equal®

Place flour, baking powder, and salt in a bowl. Blend eggs, ½ cup milk, the oil, vanilla, and ½ cup reserved blueberry juice and blend until smooth. Stir into flour mixture along with blueberries until flour is thoroughly mixed. Fill paper-lined muffin cups two-thirds full with batter. Bake in pre-heated 400° oven 20 to 25 minutes. Remove from oven and prick muffin tops in center with a fork. Using a pastry brush, glaze tops of muffins with hot milk. Roll muffin tops in bowl of Equal®.

Makes 12 muffins, 1 muffin per serving.
Calories: 115 per muffin.

Light Desserts

For me, light desserts are the best way to end meals, since they can be enjoyed without obliterating the foods served before them. I like to savor more elaborate desserts late at night or in the afternoon with tea or coffee.

This chapter begins with non-filling fruit desserts, most of which can be made in minutes. They are bright and vitamin-rich, and many are especially low in calories. There are Hot Spiced Peaches, cinnamon-scented Hot Apple Compote, and an ambrosia of tropical fruits at just 40 calories per serving—wonderful anytime!

Some of the creamy sweet-tooth satisfiers are just as calorie-carefree. These include fruity frozen yogurts, Prune Whip, Pumpkin Custard, Whipped Banana Custard, and the elegant Coupe St. Jacques. Others are thick and rich—but still as diet-wise as a 119-calorie Chocolate Mousse and 75-calorie Orange Parfaits. The molded desserts are pretty enough to please party guests. Add a topping from the Dessert Sauces chapter, and you'll forget you're on a diet!

An attractive combination with a delicious whipped topping.

Berry Compote

1 basket fresh strawberries, halved
2 bananas, sliced
½ cup white table wine
½ cup unsweetened orange juice
2 packets Equal®
½ cup plain low-fat yogurt
1 packet Equal®
1 tablespoon lemon juice

Combine fruits, wine, orange juice, and 2 packets Equal®. Mix lightly. Cover and chill 2 to 3 hours. Combine remaining ingredients; whip until smooth. Top servings of fruit and juice with yogurt mixture.

Makes 6 servings.
Calories: 87 per serving.

Try this with all the varieties of sweet apples available in autumn.

Hot Apple Compote

2 small Golden Delicious apples
1 cup water
½ cup unsweetened apple juice
1 stick cinnamon
2 orange slices, unpeeled
2 packets Equal®

64

Pare the apples and cut into fourths. Combine the water, apple juice, and cinnamon stick and simmer apples in liquid for about 2 minutes. Add the orange slices to the apples.

Bake at 300° covered, for 10 to 12 minutes or until the apples can be pierced easily with a fork. Remove from oven and stir in Equal®.

> *Makes 4 servings.*
> *Calories: 40 per serving.*

I always prepare this around the Christmas holidays because the ruby color complements the table settings and the taste is great with roast chicken.

Ruby Fruit Compote

> **2 cups water-packed pitted tart**
> **red cherries**
> **1 tablespoon cornstarch**
> **Dash salt**
> **1 tablespoon lemon juice**
> **4 drops red food coloring**
> **Dash bitters**
> **1 basket fresh whole strawberries**
> **12 packets Equal®**

Drain cherries, reserving juice. Add water to cherry juice to make 1½ cups. Blend cornstarch, salt, and cherry juice mixture. Cook, stirring till thickened and bubbly. Remove from heat and add lemon juice, food coloring, bitters, fruits, and Equal®. Mix until well blended. Chill. To serve, place ⅔ cup compote in a champagne glass.

> *Makes 6 servings.*
> *Calories: 61 per serving.*

So simple and quick to make you can serve it anytime.

Hot Spiced Peaches

8 unsweetened canned peach halves,
  undrained
1 stick cinnamon
1 clove
Pinch allspice
Pinch nutmeg
2 packets Equal®

Drain the juice from the peaches and reserve. Combine the peach juice and the spices in a small saucepan and bring to a boil. Place the peaches in a shallow baking pan and pour the juice over them; bake covered at 300° until the juice is thick, about 15 to 20 minutes. Remove from oven and add Equal®. Serve hot.

Makes 4 servings.
Calories: 40 per serving.

The coconut adds the right touch.

Strawberry Ambrosia

½ cup unsweetened coconut
1 tablespoon orange-flavored liqueur
1 basket fresh strawberries, washed
  and hulled
2 packets Equal®

66   Place coconut in bowl, sprinkle with liqueur. Mix well. Sprinkle strawberries with Equal®. Place strawberries in serving dishes and top with coconut.

Makes 6 servings.
Calories: 75 per serving.

This combination of fresh tropical fruits and citrus is lovely for a summer buffet or picnic.

Ambrosia Exotica

> 6 grapefruit sections
> 1 medium orange, peeled and
>   sectioned
> ½ cup sliced fresh pineapple
> ½ cup diced papaya
> ½ cup diced mango
> ¼ cup plain low-fat yogurt
> 2 packets Equal®
> 1 drop red food coloring (optional)

Combine the fruits in a mixing bowl and arrange the fruit into individual serving dishes. Blend the yogurt, Equal®, and food coloring together. Top each serving of fruit with some of the yogurt mixture. Serve well chilled.

Makes 6 servings.
Calories: 40 per serving.

Another fast recipe that is even good served for breakfast.

Prune Whip

> 6 ounces dietetic canned prunes,
>   with juice
> 1 teaspoon unflavored gelatin,
>   softened in warm water
> 1 teaspoon lemon juice
> ¼ teaspoon vanilla
> 1 packet Equal®
> 2 egg whites, stiffly beaten

67

In a blender, purée the prunes with the juice they are packed in. Add the softened gelatin and blend again. Simmer the purée uncovered in a heavy pan to reduce the mixture; cool slightly. Add lemon juice, vanilla, and Equal®. Gently fold the purée into the beaten egg whites. Portion the prune whip into small individual serving dishes and chill thoroughly.

Makes 6 servings.
Calories: 40 per serving.

Refreshing, thick, and creamy. You can also make lime or lemon parfaits by changing the juice and extract in this recipe.

Fruity Orange Parfaits

½ cup orange juice, unsweetened
1 teaspoon vanilla, mixed with
 ⅛ teaspoon orange extract
5 packets Equal®
2 envelopes unflavored gelatin
6 tablespoons skim milk
2 cups cottage cheese
3 egg whites
2 packets Equal®
Orange slices

Heat orange juice in a saucepan till ready to boil. Remove from heat; add vanilla and 5 packets Equal®. Pour into blender. Add gelatin and let stand for 1 minute. Whirl gelatin and juice mixture in blender until gelatin is completely dissolved. Add 3 tablespoons milk and 1 cup cottage cheese. Whip till smooth. Add remaining cup of cottage cheese, and remaining 3 tablespoons of milk. Blend until thoroughly mixed. Beat egg whites in a large bowl, adding 2 packets Equal® gradually. Beat until stiff peaks form. Add cottage cheese mixture to egg whites and fold in. Spoon into 8 parfait glasses, and chill till firm. Garnish with an orange slice, if desired.

Makes 8 servings.
Calories: 75 per serving.

A tasty way to treat an apple.

Baked Apples

**4 small baking apples
¼ cup unsweetened apple juice
1 cup water
1 teaspoon cinnamon
1 small orange, sliced
2 packets Equal®**

Preheat oven to 350°. Core the apples and remove one-fourth of the top peel. Place apples in a shallow baking pan. Combine the water, juice, and cinnamon. Pour over the apples. Arrange the orange slices around the apples to help flavor the liquid. Cover the pan with aluminum foil and bake about 20 to 30 minutes or until fork tender. Remove from oven and sprinkle with Equal®.

Makes 4 servings.
Calories: 40 per serving.

A popular summer beverage becomes a cool tangy dessert.

Sangria Orange Cups

**3 medium oranges
1¾ cups sangria (page 115)
1 package diet orange gelatin**

Mark a guideline lengthwise around middle of each orange with the tip of paring knife. Then make even scallop cuts into orange above and below line, all the way around. Pull the halves apart. Remove orange sections from orange halves with a grapefruit knife and reserve. Scoop shells clean with a large spoon. Heat sangria just to boiling in a small saucepan; stir in orange gelatin until dissolved; pour into a bowl. Chill 30 minutes or until mixture is beginning to

69

thicken. Fold orange sections and any orange juice into gelatin; chill 2 hours. Place orange shells in sherbet glasses. Spoon gelatin mixture into shells. Chill.

Makes 6 servings.
Calories: 88 per serving.

The real thing, but less fattening.

Strawberry Ice Cream

1 pint fresh strawberries
1½ teaspoons unflavored gelatin
2 tablespoons cold water 1½ cups
   heavy cream
6 packets Equal®
1½ teaspoons vanilla

Process strawberries in blender or food processor until puréed. Soften gelatin in cold water. Heat ½ cup of the cream to scalding over low heat. Add Equal® and vanilla; stir to dissolve. Add softened gelatin. Cool by placing pan in cold water. Add remaining cream and the strawberries. Blend well. Pour mixture into freezer trays, cover with transparent wrap, and freeze until firm (or pour into your ice cream maker). If in freezer for more than 6 hours before serving, allow to stand at room temperature for 15 minutes.

Makes 6 servings.
Calories: 235 per serving.

Serve with Strawberry, Soft Custard, or Butter Pecan Sauce. Delicious!

Spanish Cream

1 envelope unflavored gelatin
2 eggs, separated
2 cups skim milk
1 teaspoon vanilla
4 packets Equal®

In medium saucepan, mix gelatin and egg yolks beaten with milk. Let stand 1 minute. Stir over low heat until gelatin is completely dissolved, about 5 minutes; add vanilla. Pour into large bowl; add 2 packets Equal®. Stir occasionally until mixture mounds slightly when dropped from a spoon. In medium bowl, beat egg whites and two packets Equal® until stiff peaks form. Fold into gelatin mixture. Turn into 4-cup bowl or dessert dishes. Chill until set.

Makes 8 servings.
Calories: 63 per serving.

If you like the flavor of coffee, you'll love this one.

Coffee Custard

3 eggs
6 packets Equal®
1 envelope unflavored gelatin
2 tablespoons diet margarine, melted
1½ teaspoons instant coffee
½ teaspoon vanilla
1¼ cups skim milk
Chocolate curls for garnish (optional)

71

In blender, combine eggs, Equal®, gelatin, margarine, instant coffee, and vanilla. Blend on low speed about 30 seconds; scrape down sides. Heat milk to boiling. Cover blender, start motor, remove cover, and add hot milk; blend 10 seconds. Pour into custard dishes; chill until set, about 3 hours. Garnish with chocolate curls if desired.

Makes 4 servings.
Calories: 125 per serving.

Serve this fall favorite in tiny gourd shell for a beautiful presentation.

Pumpkin Custard

5 eggs whites
2 cups skim milk
½ teaspoon vanilla
½ cup puréed pumpkin
¼ teaspoon mace
¼ teaspoon nutmeg
¼ teaspoon cinnamon
¼ teaspoon ground cloves
6 tablespoons CinnSweet® (see page 56)

Blend the egg whites and a small amount of the milk until just combined; do not overmix. Add the remaining milk, vanilla, pumpkin, and spices, except the CinnSweet®. Blend just enough to combine the ingredients. Fill 6 warmed custard cups with the mixture. Place them in a pan of hot water and bake at 350° for 45 minutes or until set. Remove from the oven and sprinkle with CinnSweet®.

Makes 6 servings.
Calories: 40 per serving.

An easy way to enjoy a traditional homemade dessert.

Coconut Custard

3 eggs
6 packets Equal®
1 envelope unflavored gelatin
2 tablespoons diet margarine
½ teaspoon vanilla
1¼ cups skim milk
½ cup coconut, toasted

In blender, combine eggs, Equal®, gelatin, margarine, and vanilla. Blend on low speed about 30 seconds; scrape down sides. Heat milk to boiling. Cover blender, start motor, remove cover, and add hot milk; blend 10 seconds. Pour into custard dishes; chill until set, about 3 hours. Garnish with toasted coconut.

Makes 4 servings.
Calories: 181 per serving.

A classic made low-calorie.

Zabaglione and Strawberries

1½ baskets fresh strawberries
¼ cup sweet Marsala wine
4 packets Equal®
3 egg yolks

Wash and hull strawberries. If strawberries are very large, cut in half. Arrange berries in 4 wine goblets; set aside. Pour wine over Equal® in a large metal bowl that you hold over a saucepan of simmering, NOT BOILING, water. Bottom should not touch water (you can use a double boiler, but don't let the bottom of the pan touch the water or the eggs will curdle). Add egg yolks. Cook over simmering water,

73

beating constantly with an electric beater at low speed for
5 minutes, or just until mixture mounds slightly; remove
bowl from pan of water at once. Continue beating at low
speed 5 minutes longer, or until mixture is almost cold.
Pour over strawberries and serve at once. (Cover and chill
to serve later, no longer than 3 hours, so sauce holds its
airy lightness.)

Makes 4 servings.
Calories: 130 per serving.

A luscious-looking combination of cheese and fruit.

Strawberry Cheese Pudding

1 basket fresh strawberries, sliced
3 tablespoons strawberry liqueur
2 cups cottage cheese
5 eggs
¼ cup sour cream
1 teaspoon cinnamon
½ teaspoon nutmeg
¼ teaspoon ground cloves
4 packets Equal®

Preheat oven to 325°. Soak strawberries in liqueur for
1 hour. Drain and reserve liquid. In a blender, blend cottage
cheese and eggs to a smooth purée. Pour into a greased
2-quart casserole dish. Arrange strawberries on top. Bake
for 30 minutes. Meanwhile, stir remaining strawberry marinade into sour cream, cinnamon, nutmeg, cloves, and Equal®.
Spoon over strawberries and bake 10 more minutes.
Serve hot.

Makes 6 servings.
Calories: 162 per serving.

A banana dessert that's only 40 calories!

Whipped Banana Pudding

½ teaspoon unflavored gelatin,
  softened in water
1 large ripe banana
1 packet Equal®
½ teaspoon grated lemon rind
  (optional)
8 drops yellow food coloring
2 cups plain low-fat yogurt

Blend all ingredients except yogurt in a blender until smooth. Fold in the yogurt. Pour into individual sherbet glasses. Chill well.

Makes 8 servings.
Calories: 40 per serving.

Pineapple Yogurt

4 ounces low-fat yogurt (65 to 80
  calories). Use nonfat yogurt, if
  available (only 40 calories).
¼ cup coarsely chopped fresh
  pineapple
1 packet Equal®
Few drops vanilla or lemon extract
Dash cinnamon or nutmeg
2 cubes fresh pineapple

Combine yogurt with pineapple, Equal®, and flavorings to taste or top the yogurt with fresh pineapple only (handle yogurt with care because it tends to separate). Place chilled yogurt in small sherbet glasses. Garnish just before serving with fresh pineapple. Serve at once.

75

Makes 2 servings.
Calories: 40 per serving.

Tastes like ice cream but has far fewer calories.

Frozen Strawberry Yogurt

> 1 cup sliced fresh strawberries
> 1 teaspoon unflavored gelatin,
>   softened in warm water
> 1 packet Equal®
> 1 cup plain low-fat yogurt

Blend berries, softened gelatin, and Equal®. Fold into the yogurt. Pour the mixture into a shallow pan and place it in the freezer. Beat it with a fork quite frequently while it is freezing to incorporate air and also to reduce the size of the ice crystals. When it is frozen, but not too hard, it can be scooped out with an ice cream scoop and served in a sherbet glass.

> *Makes 4 servings.*
> *Calories: 40 per serving.*

This is especially nice following a main dish salad.

Frozen Blueberry Yogurt

> 1 cup frozen unsweetened blueberries
> 1 teaspoon unflavored gelatin,
>   softened in warm water
> 2 cups low-fat yogurt
> 2 packets Equal®

76 Blend the berries and softened gelatin into the yogurt; add the Equal®. Pour into a shallow pan and place in the freezer. Whip the mixture every 15 to 20 minutes with a fork until frozen, to incorporate air and to reduce the size of the ice crystals. Serve in chilled sherbet glasses.

> *Makes 8 servings.*
> *Calories: 40 per serving.*

A wonderful ending for Thanksgiving dinner.

Cranberry Frost

> 1 pound fresh cranberries
> 4 cups water
> 8 packets Equal®
> 1 teaspoon orange extract
> 1 tablespoon cranberry liqueur
> (optional)
> 1 package diet orange gelatin

Cook cranberries in water over low heat until skins pop. Strain through sieve and heat. Remove from stove, and add Equal®, flavorings, and gelatin. Stir until totally dissolved. Chill until cold, and pour into freezer trays. Freeze about 2 hours, then beat well and return to trays. Freeze until firm, about 3 hours.

> *Makes 8 servings.*
> *Calories: 64 per serving.*

Very French and very delightful. Turn this into a special occasion dessert by using it to fill Chocolate Cups (page 91).

Chocolate Mousse

> 1 envelope unflavored gelatin
> 2 cups skim milk
> 6 tablespoons semi-sweet
> chocolate chips
> 1 tablespoon cornstarch
> 1 egg, separated
> 3 packets Equal®
> 1 teaspoon vanilla
> Dash salt

77

In medium saucepan, combine gelatin and milk. Let stand 1 minute, then add chocolate chips, cornstarch, and egg yolk. Cook over medium heat, stirring constantly, until mixture comes to a full boil. Reduce heat and cook 1 minute longer. Chill until slightly thickened, stirring occasionally. Set saucepan in a larger bowl of ice cubes. Add Equal® and vanilla. Beat with mixer at high speed 5 to 6 minutes. In another bowl with clean beaters, beat egg white with salt until stiff peaks form. Fold into chocolate mixture. Spoon into 6 individual serving glasses. Chill at least 2 hours before serving.

Makes 6 servings.
Calories: 119 per serving.

A nutritious no-bake cookie.

Tropical Fruit 'n' Nut Bars

1 can (20 ounces) diet crushed
    pineapple in juice
3 envelopes unflavored gelatin
¼ cup honey
½ cup chopped walnuts
½ cup raisins
½ cup coconut
4 packets Equal®

Drain pineapple well, pressing out juice with back of spoon (reserve 1¼ cups juice). In medium saucepan, sprinkle gelatin over reserved juice; let stand 1 minute. Stir over low heat until gelatin is dissolved, about 5 minutes. Stir in honey, pineapple, and all remaining ingredients except Equal®. Remove from heat, stir in Equal®, and turn into 8- or 9-inch baking pan. Chill until firm. To serve, cut into bars.

78

Makes 12 servings
Calories: 50 per 2-bar serving.

This gourmet treat will impress all your guests. They'll never guess it's low-cal.

Coupe St. Jacques

½ teaspoon unflavored gelatin
1 cup buttermilk
¾ cup nonfat milk
1½ teaspoons vanilla
1 teaspoon grated lemon rind
½ cup chopped pitted unsweetened
   cherries
2 packets Equal®
½ cup chopped combined watermelon,
   cantaloupe, and crenshaw melon

Soften the gelatin in a few drops of water until it is completely dissolved. Combine the buttermilk, nonfat milk, and vanilla in blender. Whip the mixture to a froth; add the lemon rind, cherries, and Equal®; blend again. Place the mixture in a shallow pan and freeze to a mushy consistency. Beat the sherbet with a wire whisk or fork to get a lot of air into it and to keep the ice crystals very small. Keep whipping every 15 to 20 minutes until the sherbet is frozen. Scoop out the sherbet with an ice cream scoop. Garnish each serving with 1 tablespoon of the melon.

Makes 6 servings.
Calories: 40 per serving.

Cakes and Pies

These are luscious answers to the age-old dieter's dilemma of having your cake and eating less too. The pleasures include a raspberry-laden Fruit-Filled Cake Roll and sweet-tangy Lemon Creme Cake. For cheesecake-lovers, there's a Spicy Cheesecake that's low enough in calories to warrant adding a spoonful of Butter Pecan Sauce.

For faster satisfaction, you can quickly compose Piña Colada Crustless Pie, cherry-glazed Cherry Cheese Pie, or Key Lime Chiffon Pie. Their opulence makes these desserts look like you've spent hours in the kitchen, but none of them takes more than minutes to prepare.

When the occasion calls for more lavish efforts, you'll find spectacular cakes and pies in the Great Expectations chapter.

Fruit-Filled Cake Roll

¾ **cup all-purpose flour**
¾ **teaspoon baking powder**
¼ **teaspoon salt**
4 **eggs at room temperature**
1 **teaspoon vanilla**
3 **packets Equal®**

Filling: 1 **package diet raspberry gelatin**
1 **cup boiling water**
1 **package (10 ounces) unsweetened**
   frozen raspberries
2 **packets Equal®**

Sift flour, baking powder, and salt together. Beat eggs. Gradually fold in flour mixture; then add vanilla. Pour batter into a 15 x 10½ x 1-inch jelly-roll pan, that is sprayed with vegetable spray and lined with waxed paper which is also sprayed with vegetable spray. Bake in preheated 400° oven about 5 to 7 minutes, or until center springs back when lightly touched with fingertip. Carefully remove cake from pan by loosening edges with a knife. Invert onto a clean towel. Gently remove waxed paper, peeling from top to bottom. (Use a knife to help peel the paper.) Sprinkle with 3 packets Equal®. Roll cake beginning with short edge, using towel to support cake, rolling towel and cake together. Place seam side down on rack to cool.

Dissolve gelatin in boiling water. Add frozen fruit and stir until berries separate. Let stand until thickened, stirring occasionally. Then unroll cake, spread with filling, and roll up again. Sprinkle with 2 packets Equal® and refrigerate until ready to serve.

Makes 10 servings.
Calories: 90 per serving.

No baking—no crust—almost no calories. Light and easy.

Piña Colada Crustless Pie

6 eggs
2 envelopes unflavored gelatin
2 tablespoons diet margarine, melted
2½ cups skim milk
8 packets Equal®
2 caps coconut extract
1 cap rum extract

Topping: 1 can (8 ounces) dietetic crushed
pineapple
2 packets Equal®

In blender, combine eggs, gelatin and margarine. Blend on low speed about 30 seconds; scrape down sides. Heat milk to boiling. Cover blender, start motor, remove cover, and add hot milk slowly. Blend 10 seconds. Add 8 packets Equal® and extracts. Blend again. Spray a 9-inch glass pie plate with vegetable spray. Pour filling into pie plate and refrigerate until firm, about 6 hours. Mix pineapple and 2 packets Equal® in a small bowl. Before serving, spoon topping over pie and spread evenly.

Makes 8 servings.
Calories: 114 per serving.

Lemon Creme Cake

Filling: 5 egg yolks
1 can (14 ounces) Eagle Brand
Sweetened Condensed Milk
(NOT evaporated milk)
½ cup lemon juice
Few drops yellow food coloring,
optional
5 packets Equal®

83

Cake: **¾ cup sifted all-purpose flour**
1 teaspoon baking powder
5 eggs, separated
⅛ teaspoon salt
¼ cup lemon juice
⅛ teaspoon grated lemon rind
5 packets Equal®

Make filling first so that it has had time to set before you
begin cake. In medium bowl, beat egg yolks; stir in milk,
lemon juice, and food coloring. Add 5 packets Equal®
and beat again. Refrigerate until cake is cooled and ready
to fill.

Preheat oven to 400°. Spray 15½ x 10½ x 1-inch jelly-roll
pan with vegetable spray. Line only the bottom with waxed
paper; do not let paper come up sides of pan. Generously
spray paper with vegetable spray. Sift together flour and
baking powder onto clean piece of waxed paper. Reserve.

Beat together egg whites and salt in large bowl until soft
peaks form. Beat egg yolks with lemon juice and lemon
rind in large bowl until light and fluffy. Beat reserved flour
mixture into egg yolk mixture. Gently fold in beaten egg
whites until no streaks of white remain. Turn batter into
prepared jelly-roll pan, spreading evenly.

Bake in preheated oven for 5 to 7 minutes or until top
springs back when lightly pressed with fingertip. Cake
should not be brown. Loosen cake around edges with the tip
of a knife. Invert onto a clean towel. Very carefully peel
off paper. (Use knife to help peel off waxed paper.) Starting
at short end, roll up cake and towel together. Place roll,
seam side down, on rack. Cool completely. When jelly roll is
cool, unroll carefully. Sprinkle with 5 packets Equal®.
Spread roll evenly with filling; reroll without the towel. Place
roll, seam side down, on a serving plate. Refrigerate, covered, until ready to serve. Garnish with remaining lemon
creme, if desired.

84   *Makes 10 servings.*
Calories: 155 per serving.

Cherry Cheese Pie

Graham Cracker Crust:
> **1 cup graham cracker crumbs**
> **2 tablespoons diet margarine, melted**
> **2 packets Equal®**

Cherry Glaze:
> **1 can (16 ounces) dietetic red sour**
> **pitted cherries**
> **2 teaspoons cornstarch**
> **3 packets Equal®**
> **⅛ teaspoon almond extract**
> **8 drops red food coloring (optional)**

Cheese Filling:
> **1 teaspoon unflavored gelatin**
> **1 tablespoon cold water**
> **1¼ cups low-fat cottage cheese**
> **½ teaspoon vanilla**
> **3 packets Equal®**

Make graham cracker crust: combine crumbs with diet margarine and 2 packets Equal® by cutting in melted margarine until mixture resembles coarse crumbs. Press firmly in bottom and sides of 8- or 9-inch pie plate. Refrigerate until ready to use.

Make cherry glaze: drain cherries, reserving liquid. In a small saucepan, combine cornstarch and reserved cherry liquid; stir until smooth. Cook over medium heat, stirring constantly, until mixture comes to a boil. Reduce heat and cook 1 minute longer. Remove from heat; stir in cherries. Let cool to lukewarm, then stir in 3 packets Equal®, almond extract, and coloring.

Make cheese filling: combine gelatin and cold water in small bowl; let stand 1 minute. Set bowl in ½ inch boiling water. Heat just until gelatin is dissolved. Remove from water; let cool slightly. In blender, combine cottage cheese and vanilla. Blend until smooth. With motor running, gradually add the dissolved gelatin. Transfer to bowl and add 3 packets Equal®. Chill, stirring occasionally, just until slightly thickened, about 20 minutes.

85

Fill pie crust with cheese filling. Wait until pie is firm, about 3 hours, and spread cherry glaze on top. Refrigerate until ready to serve.

Makes 6 servings.
Calories: 184 per serving.

Key Lime Chiffon Pie

1 graham cracker crust (page 85)

Filling: **1 envelope unflavored gelatin**
¼ cup cold water
4 eggs, separated
2 teaspoons grated lime peel
½ cup lime juice
¼ teaspoon salt
6 packets Equal®
2 to 3 drops green food coloring
4 packets Equal®

Make graham cracker crust (see page 85). Stir gelatin into cold water. Beat egg yolks lightly in small saucepan. Stir in lime peel, juice, and salt. Cook over medium heat, stirring constantly, 6 to 8 minutes or until mixture is slightly thickened. Remove from heat: add gelatin. Stir until gelatin dissolves. Stir in 6 packets Equal®. Mix in food coloring a drop at a time. Chill in refrigerator until mixture mounds slightly when dropped from a spoon, about 25 to 40 minutes. Beat egg whites until frothy. Add 4 packets Equal® gradually, beating constantly until stiff peaks form. Spread over gelatin; fold in whites. Spoon into crust; chill until firm.

Makes 1 9-inch pie, or 6 servings
Calories: 145 per serving.

Serve basic cheesecake plain, topped with fruit, or with a delicious sauce, such as warm Butter Pecan Sauce (page 103).

Spicy Cheesecake

> 1 container (16 ounces) low-fat
>   cottage cheese
> 2 eggs
> 4 tablespoons instant nonfat dry
>   milk powder
> 1 teaspoon vanilla
> ½ teaspoon grated lemon rind
> 2 egg whites
> ¼ teaspoon cream of tartar
> 1 cup CinnSweet® (see page 56)

Spray bottom and side of 8-inch springform pan with vegetable spray. Preheat oven to 350°. Combine cottage cheese, eggs, 2 tablespoons of the milk powder, the vanilla and lemon rind in blender; cover. Whirl until smooth, scraping down sides as necessary. Beat egg whites with cream of tartar in a medium bowl until foamy. Gradually beat in remaining 2 tablespoons of milk powder. Continue beating until soft peaks form. Fold egg whites into cheese mixture until no streaks of white remain. Pour mixture into prepared pan. Bake in preheated oven for 35 minutes or until top is browned and a wooden toothpick comes out clean when inserted into the center. Top with CinnSweet® sprinkled over cake like a blanket.

Makes 8 servings.
Calories: 90 per serving.

Great Expectations

Desserts are an important part of celebrating the special moments of our lives. Whether it's a birthday, holiday, or the first day of spring, a dramatic dessert marks the specialness of the occasion.

You don't have to throw calorie-caution to the wind to join these celebrations. As proof of this, I offer recipes for Espresso Parfait Cheesecake, Strawberry Mousse in Chocolate Cups, and an elegant Black Forest Cake Roll. There are cream puffs, meringues, and two beautiful molded creations—Pineapple-Rice Cream and Strawberry Bavarian Creme. And for the Yuletide season, there's my low-calorie version of the classic French Bûche de Noel.

All of these look as tantalizing as they taste. So serve them on your most attractive china or crystal to fulfill every guest's Great Expectations.

This cheesecake takes a little time but it's worth it. A nice way to end a special meal.

Espresso Parfait Cheesecake

Crust:
**1 cup finely crushed zwieback
2 tablespoons diet margarine, melted
1 tablespoon honey**

Filling:
**1 envelope unflavored gelatin
¼ cup water
2 egg yolks, beaten
½ cup skim milk
⅓ cup ricotta cheese
2 teaspoons instant espresso coffee
   (regular instant can also be used)
1 teaspoon vanilla
⅓ cup water
2 packets Equal®
1 envelope diet dessert topping mix
½ cup skim milk
4 egg whites
2 packets Equal®**

Combine zwieback, margarine, and honey. Reserve 2 table-spoons of the mixture for topping. Press remaining mixture onto bottom of sprayed (use vegetable spray) 7- or 8-inch springform pan. Chill. Soften gelatin in ¼ cup water. In a saucepan, combine egg yolks, ½ cup milk, the ricotta, coffee crystals, vanilla, and ⅓ cup of water. Stir in gelatin mixture. Cook and stir over medium heat 20 minutes or until mixture coats a spoon; do NOT boil. Remove from heat and stir in 2 packets Equal®. Chill until partially set, stirring occasionally.

Prepare topping mix according to package directions, using ½ cup milk. Fold into gelatin mixture. Beat egg whites, and 2 packets Equal® until they form stiff peaks. Add to gelatin mixture by folding in gently. Turn into prepared pan; cover and chill till firm, about 6 hours. To serve, remove the sides of pan and sprinkle with reserved cracker crumbs.

90

*Makes 10 servings.
Calories: 133 per serving.*

A romantically beautiful dessert that's easy to make.

Strawberry Mousse in Chocolate Cups

6 squares semisweet chocolate
1 tablespoon vegetable oil
1 package (10 ounces) unsweetened
   frozen strawberries, thawed
1½ envelopes unflavored gelatin
3 packets Equal®
2 egg whites
2 packets Equal®
1 cup whipped diet dessert
   topping mix

Melt chocolate with oil shortening in top of double boiler over hot water. Remove from heat, but keep pan over warm water. Using a pastry brush, spread thin layer of chocolate over insides of 12 pleated foil cupcake liners. Refrigerate 1 hour or until firm. Coat a second time. (Any extra chocolate may be used for dipping strawberries.) Gently peel foil from cups; keep refrigerated until ready to fill. Purée strawberries in blender. Transfer to a saucepan, and sprinkle gelatin over top. Place over low heat; stir to dissolve gelatin. Transfer to large bowl. Place over ice water, stirring often, until mixture begins to thicken. Add 3 packets Equal® and mix thoroughly. Beat egg whites until foamy. Beat in 2 packets Equal®, and continue beating until stiff peaks form. Fold whipped topping mix, then egg whites, into strawberry mixture. Spoon mixture into each chocolate cup. Chill.

Makes 12 servings.
Calories: 97 per serving.

Custard in Meringue Shells

Coffee Custard or Coconut Custard
(see Index)

Meringue Shells:
> 4 egg whites
> Pinch of salt
> 4 teaspoons crème de cacao
> 2 packets Equal®

Make custard. Chill in bowl until set.

Place egg whites and salt in bowl. Beat together until frothy. Gradually add crème de cacao. Continue beating until whites are stiff, glossy, and stand in stiff peaks. Spray a six-muffin tin with vegetable spray. Fill cups with meringue, hollowing out top with back of spoon. Bake at 250° for 1 hour. Remove from oven and dust with Equal®. Fill with custard; refrigerate.

> *Makes 6 meringues.*
> *Calories: 28 each.*

Tip: Beating Egg Whites for Meringues:
Egg whites will beat better at room temperature, but eggs separate more easily when cold. So the trick is to separate them when cold, and then let them stand until they reach room temperature. The best way to beat egg whites is with a hand electric beater; however, a rotary beater will also do the job.

Strawberry Bavarian Cream

92

> 1 pint fresh strawberries, hulled
> 2 eggs, separated
> 1 envelope unflavored gelatin
> 6 packets Equal®
> 1 tablespoon fresh lemon juice
> ½ teaspoon vanilla
> 1 packet Equal®

1 cup heavy cream
Whole strawberries for garnish
(optional)

Place strawberries in blender or food processor. Cover; whirl until puréed. Combine ¾ cup of the purée with egg yolks in medium saucepan. Stir in gelatin and 6 packets Equal®. Place over low heat; stir until gelatin and Equal® are dissolved. Transfer to a medium bowl. Stir in remaining strawberry purée, lemon juice, and vanilla. Set bowl in large bowl of ice and water. Refrigerate, stirring occasionally, until mixture mounds slightly when spooned, about 30 minutes. Beat egg whites in small bowl until foamy. Beat in 1 packet Equal®, half at a time, until meringue forms soft peaks. Fold into strawberry mixture. Without washing bowl or beaters, beat cream in bowl until soft peaks form. Fold into strawberry mixture. Rinse a 5-cup mold with cold water; shake out excess. Pour strawberry mixture into mold. Gently tap mold on counter to settle mixture. Smooth top with spatula. Refrigerate until set, 4 to 6 hours.

To serve, very briefly dip the mold into bowl of warm water. Invert serving dish over mold; turn right side up. Gently shake mold to loosen; carefully remove mold. Garnish with strawberry slices if desired.

Makes 8 servings.
Calories: 200 per serving.

Molded Pineapple-Rice Cream

⅓ cup raw regular white rice
2½ cups skim milk
½ teaspoon salt
2 envelopes plain gelatin
1 cup diet crushed pineapple,
 undrained
8 packets Equal®
⅓ cup flaked coconut
1 teaspoon vanilla

93

½ teaspoon almond extract
1 cap pineapple extract
1 cup cottage cheese whipped in
   blender with 1 packet Equal®
4 canned diet pineapple slices, halved

In top of double boiler, combine rice, milk and salt. Cook over boiling water, covered and stirring occasionally until rice is tender, about 1 hour and 15 minutes. In small bowl, sprinkle gelatin over crushed pineapple; let stand 5 minutes to soften. Turn into hot rice mixture, stirring to dissolve gelatin completely. Add 8 packets Equal®. Stir in coconut, vanilla, and almond and pineapple extracts. Refrigerate until cool, about 1 hour. Mixture should be firm enough to mound. With rubber scraper, fold whipped cottage cheese into cooled gelatin mixture, mixing thoroughly. Spray a 1½-quart mold with vegetable spray. Turn mixture into mold and refrigerate until firm, at least 3 hours or overnight. To unmold, run a sharp knife around edge of mold to loosen. Invert on serving platter; shake to unmold. Arrange pineapple slices round side up all along edge of mold.

Makes 8 servings.
Calories: 119 per serving.

This is one of my favorite recipes. You can fill the plain puffs with crab, salmon, or shrimp salad for a luncheon or appetizer. Here they are the basis for a spectacular dessert.

Miniature Cream Puffs with Mocha Filling

½ cup butter or diet margarine
1 cup water
⅛ teaspoon salt
1 cup flour
4 eggs

Mocha Filling:

1 envelope diet dessert topping mix
2 teaspoons instant coffee crystals
4 packets Equal®
5 packets Equal®

In heavy 2-quart saucepan, combine butter, water, and salt. Bring to a boil; remove from heat; stir in flour vigorously with wooden spoon until mixture forms a firm ball. Return to medium-low heat; cook and stir 1 minute or until ball leaves the sides of pan. Cool 5 minutes. Beat in eggs, one at a time, beating well after each, until dough is smooth and glossy. On lightly sprayed baking sheets (use vegetable spray), drop slightly rounded measuring teaspoonsfull 2 inches apart. Bake, 1 sheet at a time, in preheated 425° oven 15 to 20 minutes, or until puffs are golden brown. Remove to racks to cool. Cut tops off puffs; fill as desired; replace tops.

Mocha Filling: Prepare whipped topping according to package directions; add coffee and Equal®. Fill cream puffs with 1 tablespoon filling and replace tops. Arrange puffs on plate, pyramid style. Sift 5 packets Equal® over top. (One envelope of topping mix will fill about 32 puffs. Double the recipe for filling if you are planning to use all the puffs in this recipe for 1 dessert.)

Makes 78 puffs.
Calories: 18 per puff; 90 per 3-puff serving
*   with mocha filling.*

Tip: Store leftover unfilled puffs in an airtight container. Heat in low oven or microwave oven (very briefly, or they'll harden!) to recrisp.

Guests love this low-cal version of a bake-shop classic. Cherries and chocolate are an all-time crowd pleaser.

Black Forest Cake Roll

Filling: 1 can (8 ounces) dietetic red sour
       pitted cherries
1 teaspoon cornstarch
2 packets Equal®
1/8 teaspoon almond extract
Few drops red food coloring (optional)

Cake: 3/4 cup sifted all-purpose flour
1 teaspoon baking powder
5 eggs, separated
1/8 teaspoon salt
1/2 cup brewed coffee
1/3 cup cocoa
10 packets Equal®
1 envelope diet dessert topping mix
       (makes 2 cups)

Make filling first so that it is firm enough to spread.

Drain cherries, reserving liquid and a few cherries for garnish. In small saucepan combine cornstarch and reserved liquid; stir until smooth. Cook over medium heat, stirring constantly, until mixture comes to a boil. Reduce heat and cook 1 minute longer. Remove from heat and stir in cherries. Let cool to lukewarm, then stir in Equal®, almond extract, and color. Refrigerate while you are making cake.

Preheat oven to 400°. Spray 15½ x 10½ x 1-inch jelly-roll pan with vegetable spray. Line only the bottom of the pan with waxed paper and spray with vegetable spray. Sift together flour and baking powder onto clean piece of waxed paper. Reserve. Beat together egg whites and salt in large bowl until soft peaks form. Beat egg yolks with coffee until light and fluffy. Add cocoa and beat again. Beat in reserved flour mixture. Gently fold in beaten egg whites until no streaks of white remain. Turn batter into prepared jelly-roll pan, spreading evenly. Bake for 5 to 7 minutes, or until top springs back when lightly pressed with fingertip. Loosen cake around edges with knife. Invert onto clean towel. Very carefully peel off paper using knife to help peel paper, if necessary. Sprinkle cake with 10 packets Equal®. Starting at short end, roll up cake and towel together. Place seam side down on rack to cool.

Meanwhile prepare dessert topping mix according to package directions; reserve ¼ cup. Unroll cake and spread remaining topping mix evenly, leaving a 1-inch border around edge of cake. Spoon cherry filling on top of whipped topping, being careful to spread evenly. Do not fill cake too much or filling will seep out when you reroll cake. Reroll cake without the towel. Place seam side down on serving plate and top with reserved whipped topping. Garnish with cherries, if desired.

Makes 10 servings.
Calories: 107 per serving.

No French Christmas celebration would be complete without a Bûche de Noel, the traditional Christmas cake baked and decorated to look like a Yule log. This is a low-calorie version, perfect for a party.

Bûche De Noel

¾ cup sifted all-purpose flour
1 teaspoon baking powder
5 eggs, separated
⅛ teaspoon salt
½ cup brewed coffee
⅓ cup unsweetened cocoa
10 packets Equal®

Filling: 1 envelope diet dessert topping mix
           (makes 2 cups)
½ cup cold water
1 teaspoon vanilla
¼ cup unsweetened cocoa
2 teaspoons instant coffee crystals
8 packets Equal®

97

Equal® and cherries for garnish
(optional)

Spray bottom of a 15½ x 10½ x 1-inch jelly-roll pan. Spray
with vegetable spray. Line bottom with waxed paper. Spray
with vegetable spray. Preheat oven to 400°. Sift together flour
and baking powder onto a piece of waxed paper. Reserve.
 In a large bowl, at high speed, beat egg whites with salt
until stiff peaks form. Beat egg yolks with coffee and cocoa
till well blended. Beat in reserved flour mixture. Gently fold
in beaten egg whites until no white streaks remain. Turn
batter into prepared jelly-roll pan and bake 5 to 7 minutes.
Test cake by tapping center with your fingertip; cake should
spring back when done. Remove from oven and loosen cake
around edges with knife. Invert onto a clean towel and
peel the paper from the cake carefully. Use a knife to help
peel off paper. Sprinkle cake with 10 packets of Equal®.
Starting with short end, roll up cake and towel together.
Place roll seam side down on rack. Cool. Meanwhile
prepare filling.
 Combine topping mix and cold water in a mixing bowl.
Beat at high speed until topping is thick and fluffy. Add
vanilla, cocoa, coffee, and 8 packets Equal®. Continue beating until well blended. Unroll jelly roll and spread with filling. Reroll without the towel and place seam side down
on serving plate. Garnish with Equal® sprinkled on top to
resemble snow and cherries, if desired.

Makes 10 servings.
Calories: 101 per serving.

Savory Sauces, Dessert Sauces, Jellies, and Jams

Without a sauce, many dishes would be sadly lacking. In the past, dieters have avoided such dishes because they believed the sauce added unnecessary calories. But I see no reason to pass up a shrimp cocktail with a tangy dipping sauce, spareribs with a robust barbecue sauce, or Oriental-style fare with a sweet and sour sauce. All of these can be enjoyed by substituting recipes in this chapter for higher-calorie versions.

There's no need to pass up sweet toppings either. You can look forward to pudding or plain cake with Soft Custard Sauce, rum flavored Eggnog Sauce, or warm Butter Pecan Sauce. A simple fruit cup will look extravagant if you add less than 20 calories worth of Orange Sauce or Strawberry Sauce. Take saucemaking a step further and you get the freshest-tasting jellies and jams to spread on morning toast or dinner crêpes. The flavors of these preserves, like those of the sauces, will always outshine those of commercial blends, simply because they're homemade from the best ingredients.

Brush on broiled or roasted chicken, and place remaining sauce in cup for dipping. It can also be used to sauce cocktail franks and appetizer meatballs.

Spicy Barbecue Sauce

1½ tablespoons diet margarine
¾ cup chopped onion
1½ cups dietetic ketchup
1 cup plus 2 tablespoons vinegar
¾ cup diet pancake syrup
¾ cup water
3 beef bouillon cubes
1½ tablespoons Worcestershire sauce
2¼ teaspoons salt
¼ teaspoon pepper
3 drops Tabasco sauce
1 packet Equal®

Melt margarine in saucepan. Add onion and sauté until lightly browned. Then add remaining ingredients except Equal®. Boil slowly 15 minutes, or until sauce is glossy and thick. Remove from heat and stir in Equal®.

Makes 2¼ cups.
Calories: 10 per tablespoon.

Sweet and Sour Sauce

1 tablespoon cornstarch
⅓ cup chicken broth
⅓ cup red wine vinegar
2 tablespoons frozen concentrated
    pineapple juice
2 tablespoons chopped pimiento
1 tablespoon soy sauce
¼ teaspoon garlic powder
¼ teaspoon ground ginger
2 packets Equal®

Combine cornstarch and chicken broth in small saucepan. Stir in all remaining ingredients except Equal®. Cook over medium heat, stirring, until thickened and bubbly. Remove from heat and stir in Equal®. Serve warm.

Makes 1 cup.
Calories: 5 per tablespoon.

Add 2 small chopped green chilies to turn this relish into a zesty taco sauce with a chunky texture.

Tomato Relish

2 medium tomatoes, finely chopped
½ minced onion
½ cup minced green pepper
¼ cup cider vinegar
2 tablespoons chopped fresh basil leaves or 2 teaspoons dried crushed basil leaves
1 packet Equal®
Salt and pepper to taste (optional)

In a medium bowl, combine all ingredients. Relish may be used at once or stored in sealed refrigerator container up to 1 week.

Makes 1 cup, or four ¼-cup servings.
Calories: 35 per serving.

Carole's Spa Cocktail Sauce

101

1 bottle (11 ounces) dietetic ketchup (no sugar or salt)
1 tablespoon freshly squeezed lemon juice

¼ cup horseradish
¼ cup chopped celery
2 packets Equal®
¼ cup chopped chives (optional)

Mix the first three ingredients in the order given. (Adjust lemon and horseradish to taste.) Stir in Equal® and celery. Refrigerate covered. Serve very hot or very cold. Add fresh chives just before serving if desired.

Makes 2 cups.
Calories: 10 per tablespoon.

This light sauce is delicious served over cake or pudding.

Soft Custard Sauce

3 egg yolks
Pinch salt
1 cup scalded skim milk
¼ teaspoon vanilla
2 packets Equal®

Beat egg yolks slightly. Add salt and mix well. Stir in scalded milk. Cook and stir over hot water until mixture coats a spoon. Remove from heat; stir in vanilla and Equal®.

Makes 1¼ cups.
Calories: 14 per tablespoon.

Variations:

Rum Sauce: Add 1 cap rum extract to basic Soft Custard
102   Sauce recipe.
Almond Sauce: Add 1 cap almond extract to basic recipe.
Lemon Sauce: Add 1 cap lemon extract to basic recipe.
Brandy Sauce: Add 1 cap brandy extract to basic recipe.
Coconut Sauce: Add 1 cap coconut extract to basic recipe.

To top ice cream, crêpes, or pudding—and especially good served warm.

Butter Pecan Sauce

> **1 cup diet pancake syrup**
> **1 cap butter extract**
> **Dash salt**
> **½ cup skim milk**
> **½ packet Equal®**
> **½ cup chopped pecans**

Boil syrup until a small amount forms a soft ball in cold water (or to a temperature of 236°). Remove from heat and add butter extract and salt. Stir well and cool. Add milk, Equal®, and pecans.

> *Makes 1 ¾ cups sauce.*
> *Calories: 20 per tablespoon.*

Strawberry Sauce

> **2 cups fresh strawberries (frozen can**
>   **be used, but thaw first)**
> **2 teaspoons cornstarch**
> **4 packets Equal®**

Place strawberries in blender and blend till berries are mashed. Place mashed berries in a small saucepan and add cornstarch. Cook over medium heat until mixture boils, stirring constantly. Remove from heat and stir in Equal®. Refrigerate sauce until well chilled.

103

> *Makes 1¼ cups.*
> *Calories: 5 calories per tablespoon.*

Tip: Substitute peaches, pineapple, cherries, blueberries, or raspberries, for the strawberries, if you wish.

Serve on fruit, plain cake, pudding, or ice cream.

Orange Sauce

> **3 tablespoons cornstarch**
> **Dash salt**
> **1⅓ cups hot water**
> **3 packets Equal®**
> **4 teaspoons diet margarine**
> **½ cup quick-frozen concentrated**
>   **orange juice**

Combine cornstarch and salt in a saucepan. Add hot water gradually, stirring constantly. Cook and stir over medium heat until thick and somewhat clear, about 5 minutes. Remove from heat and stir in Equal® and margarine. Blend in concentrated orange juice. Blend till smooth.

> *Makes 2 cups.*
> *Calories: 11 per tablespoon.*

Wonderful on vanilla ice cream or puddings.

Eggnog Sauce

> **1 tablespoon flour**
> **Dash salt**
> **1 egg, separated**
> **1¼ cups skim milk**
> **2 packets Equal®**
> **⅛ teaspoon nutmeg**
> **1 cap rum extract**
> **1 packet Equal®**

104

Combine the flour, and salt in top of double boiler. Add egg yolk and beat well. Gradually add milk, stirring constantly. Cook over rapidly boiling water 5 minutes, stirring occasionally. Remove from heat and add 2 packets Equal® and nutmeg. Blend, then add rum extract. Blend again. Cool.

Beat egg white until foamy. Add remaining packet of Equal®
to egg white, beating constantly until mixture will stand
in soft peaks. Fold in egg yolk mixture.

Makes 2 cups.
Calories: 8 per tablespoon.

This is my favoarite on any muffin or toast. It makes a nice
Christmas gift for friends—present it in small decorative
jelly jars.

The Best Marmalade

4 oranges
2 lemons
1 grapefruit
2 cups cold water
2 tablespoons orange-flavored liqueur
2 teaspoons cinnamon
3 packets Equal®

Slice oranges, lemons, and grapefruit into very thin slices.
Place in a saucepan. Add cold water; cover and boil gently
for 2 hours. Uncover, add liqueur , and simmer for 1 hour
more. Cool; add cinnamon and Equal®. Spoon into sterilized
jars. Refrigerate.

Makes 4 cups.
Calories: 7 per tablespoon.

Rhubarb Strawberry Jelly

105

5 large stalks rhubarb
½ cup water
1 package diet strawberry gelatin

**1 cup fresh strawberries, halved
and sliced
4 packets Equal®**

Cut off leaves and stem ends from rhubarb. Wash thoroughly. Dry well. If rhubarb is young, the skin is tender and will not need to be peeled. If skin is tough, peel rhubarb. Cut rhubarb into ½-inch pieces. Place in large saucepan with water. Bring to a boil. Lower heat and simmer, covered, for 15 minutes. Stir in gelatin and strawberries. Remove from heat and cool 10 minutes. Stir in Equal®. Spoon into sterilized jars. Chill until set. Keep refrigerated.

Makes about 2 cups.
Calories: 4 per tablespoon.

Berry Jam

**1 tablespoon unflavored gelatin
1 cup cold water
½ cup strawberries
½ cup raspberries
½ cup blueberries
Juice of ½ lime
2 packets Equal®**

Add gelatin to cold water. Bring to a boil, stirring until completely dissolved. Cool gelatin in refrigerator until it reaches consistency of egg white. Heat berries in saucepan for about 5 minutes, or until tender. Remove from heat and crush berries with a fork. Stir for 2 minutes to cool. Add lime juice and Equal® to berries. Stir well. Fold berries into thickened gelatin. Mix well. Spoon into sterilized jars. Chill until jellied. Keep refrigerated.

106

Makes 2 cups.
Calories: 4 per tablespoon.

Tip: Jams and jellies will keep refrigerated up to 1 month— if you don't eat them first! They make delicious dessert toppings and fillings for crêpes.

Beverages

These are some pleasures that no dieter need miss: A frosty glass of lemonade on a sultry summer day. A steaming cup of hot spiced tea on a blustery December afternoon. A perfect cup of cappuccino to end a wonderful dinner. A thick, rich shake to appease between-meal appetites. A sociable cocktail to share with guests.

In the pages that follow you'll find low-calorie versions of these drinks and many more. The recipes are quick, easy, and as mouthwatering as Piña Colada, Sangria, and a Chocolate Shake. They're suitable for single servings or party punch bowls, so you can enjoy the sipping anytime.

This is the basic thick, rich milk shake. Be sure to include the ice cubes in all the variations that follow, because the cubes are needed for volume and thickness.

Vanilla Shake

½ cup skim milk
3 packets Equal®
1 teaspoon vanilla extract
3 ice cubes

Place all ingredients in blender. Using high speed, blend for about 2 minutes, or until ice cubes are melted.

Makes 1 serving.
Calories: 71.

Variations:

You'll feel like you're in the tropics.

Piña Colada
Add 1½ tablespoons drained, crushed pineapple (packed in unsweetened juice). Substitute 1 teaspoon rum extract for vanilla. Add 1 cap of coconut extract. Proceed as above.

Calories: 93.

Maple Walnut Creme
Substitute 1 cap maple extract and 1 cap black walnut extract for vanilla. Proceed as above.

Calories: 75.

108

Butter Almond Creme

Substitute 1 cap butter extract and 1 cap almond extract for vanilla. Proceed as above.

Calories: 78.

This is my favorite. For a more intense chocolate taste, add ½ cap chocolate extract.

Chocolate Shake

> ½ cup skim milk
> 3 packets Equal®
> 2 teaspoons cocoa
> ½ teaspoon vanilla
> 3 ice cubes

Place all ingredients in blender. Using high speed, blend for about 2 minutes, or until ice cubes are melted.

Makes 1 serving.
Calories: 71.

Variations:

By adding an egg to the Mocha shake, you have a terrific way to start the day.

Mocha
Substitute 1 ½ teaspoons instant coffee and ½ cap mocha extract for vanilla. Proceed as above.

Calories: 75.

Chocolate Cherry
Substitute 1 cap cherry extract for vanilla. Proceed as above.

Calories: 81.

Chocolate Mint
109
Substitute ¼ cap of mint extract for vanilla extract. Proceed as before.

Calories: 71.

Chocolate Coconut

Substitute 1 cap coconut extract for vanilla. Proceed as above.

Calories: 81.

Chocolate Rum Coconut

Substitute 1 cap rum and ½ cap coconut extract for vanilla. Proceed as above.

Calories: 83.

This drink is an excellent high-protein way to start the day.

Coffee-Maple Breakfast Protein

1 cup brewed coffee
1 tablespoon maple extract
2 tablespoons sour cream
1 packet Equal®
2 eggs
1 tablespoon liquid lecithin
1 teaspoon brewer's yeast
6 ice cubes

Place all ingredients in blender and blend until smooth.

Makes 1 serving.
Calories: 246.

This is a great staple. So refreshing, and almost no calories.

Iced Tea

¾ cup brewed tea
2 packets Equal®
Lemon slice

Combine tea and Equal®. Stir and add ice cubes. Garnish with lemon.

Makes one 6-ounce serving.
Calories: 11.

Another great summer beverage.

Iced Coffee

¾ cup brewed coffee
1 tablespoon skim milk
2 packets Equal®

Combine coffee, skim milk and Equal®. Add ice cubes and stir.

Makes one 6-ounce serving.
Calories: 15.

For me, the most comforting drink on a busy day.

Cappuccino

1 cup skim milk, heated
1½ teaspoons instant coffee
Few drops brandy extract

2 packets Equal®
Dash of cinnamon

Heat milk, and add remaining ingredients except cinnamon. Top with cinnamon.

Makes 1 serving.
Calories: 112.

Summer Orange Tea

¾ cup brewed tea
1 packet Equal®
2 teaspoons orange juice
1 cinnamon stick
Orange slice

Combine tea, Equal®, and orange juice. Add ice cubes and stir with cinnamon stick. Garnish with orange slice.

Makes one 6-ounce serving.
Calories: 14.

Lemonade

¼ cup lemon juice
4 packets Equal®
¾ cup water
Ice cubes
Lemon slice

Combine lemon juice and Equal® in tall glass. Add water and ice cubes. Garnish with lemon.

Makes one 8-ounce serving.
Calories: 32.

These cocktails have the great taste of alcoholic beverages without the calories. You can mix whole pitchers of them when you are entertaining.

Mock Sour

2 cups orange juice
¼ cup lemon juice
6 packets Equal®
¼ cup water
8 ice cubes
1 cap rum extract

Combine all ingredients except rum extract in blender. Blend for 1 minute. Add rum extract and blend again. Pour into 4 glasses and serve.

Makes 4 servings.
Calories: 65 per serving.

Virgin Mary

6 ounces V-8 Juice or tomato juice
1 tablespoon horseradish
Squeeze of lemon or lime
Dash Worcestershire sauce
Dash pepper
½ packet Equal®
1 stalk celery

Place all ingredients except celery into blender and blend for 1 minute. Pour into chilled glasses with ice cubes and garnish with celery.

113

Makes one 6-ounce serving.
Calories: 96.

Mock Champagne

2¼ cups unsweetened pineapple juice
2 tablespoons lime juice
2 packets Equal®
4 ounces club soda, chilled
Lime twists

Combine pineapple and lime juices with Equal® and chill. Just before serving, pour juice mixture into eight 4-ounce champagne glasses. Add a lime twist to each, and fill glasses slowly with soda.

Makes 8 servings.
Calories: 35 per serving.

The rich ruby color of this drink makes it ideal for holiday entertaining.

Cranberry Cocktail

½ cup low-calorie cranberry juice
Juice of ¼ lemon
2 packets Equal®
½ cap of rum extract
Orange slice

Combine all ingredients except orange slice in a mixing glass. Shake with crushed ice and pour into a glass. Garnish with orange slice.

Makes one 6-ounce serving.
Calories: 80.

Always welcome at a party.

Sangria

1 bottle (1 quart) claret wine, chilled
1 cup unsweetened pineapple juice,
chilled
12 packets Equal®
1 cup fresh pineapple chunks
½ orange, thinly sliced and quartered
2 bottles (10 ounces each) club soda

Combine wine, juice, and Equal® in pitcher. Add fruit and soda. Mix well and serve immediately in wineglasses.

Makes thirteen ½-cup servings.
Calories: 76 per serving.

This is another soothing beverage, and one that can be served for holiday entertaining. Just multiply the servings and mix the tea in a wassail bowl. Sprinkle a few whole cloves on top.

Hot Spiced Tea

¾ cup brewed tea
1 packet Equal®
2 teaspoons orange juice
1 cinnamon stick
Orange slice

Combine hot tea, Equal®, and orange juice in a cup. Stir with cinnamon stick and garnish with orange slice.

115

Makes one 6-ounce serving.
Calories: 14.

Brand Index

I suggest using the following products when called for in the *Free and Equal®* recipes because I find them to be the lowest in calories or believe the taste to be better than others. These are the product names and the manufacturers.

Gelatin and Whipped Topping Mix: *D-Zerta,* distributed by General Foods Corp., 250 North Street, White Plains, New York.

Tomato products: packed by Hunt Wesson, Fullerton, California.

Worcestershire Sauce: manufactured by Lea & Perrins, 1501 Pollitt Drive, Fair Lawn, New Jersey.

Vegetable Spray: *Pam* vegetable cooking spray, distributed by Boyle-Midway, Inc., 685 Third Avenue, New York, New York. Pam may be purchased in the cooking oil department of your supermarket.

Extracts: *Wagner's Extracts,* distributed by John Wagner & Sons, Inc., Soyland, Pennsylvania.

Mayonnaise and Margarine: *Weight Watchers* brand, distributed by Nutrition Industries Corp., Cresskill, New Jersey.

Dietetic Cream Cheese: Kraft Inc., Glenview, Illinois.

Cooking and Salad Oil: *Mazola Corn Oil,* manufactured by Best Foods, CPC International Inc., General Offices, Englewood Cliffs, New Jersey.

Pancake Syrup; Imitation Ketchup: *Featherweight* brand, manufactured by Chicago Dietetic Supply Inc., La Grange, Illinois.   117

Pork Rinds: *Jays* brand, distributed by Jays Foods Inc., Chicago, Illinois. Pork rinds may be purchased in the potato chip and pretzel department of your supermarket.

Dietetic Spaghetti: *Thin Spaghetti,* manufactured by the Prince Company Inc., Spaghettiville, Lowell, Massachussetts.

Index

119

Index

Index

122

Notes & Recipes